SAY I'M DEAD

SAY I'M DEAD

~ *A Family Memoir* ~

OF RACE, SECRETS, AND LOVE

E. DOLORES JOHNSON

Lawrence Hill Books

Chicago

Published by Lawrence Hill Books
An imprint of Chicago Review Press Incorporated
814 North Franklin Street
Chicago, Illinois 60610
ISBN 978-1-64160-274-7

Library of Congress Cataloging-in-Publication Data

Names: Johnson, E. Dolores, author.
Title: Say I'm dead : a family memoir of race, secrets, and love / E. Dolores Johnson.
Other titles: Family memoir of race, secrets, and love
Description: Chicago : Lawrence Hill Books, [2020] | Summary: "Fearful of violating
    Indiana's anti-miscegenation laws in the 1940s, E. Dolores Johnson's black
    father and white mother fled Indianapolis to secretly marry. Johnson searched
    her father's black genealogy and then was amazed to suddenly realize that her
    mother's whole white side was missing in family history. Johnson went searching
    for the white family who did not know she existed. When she found them, it's
    not just their shock and her mother's shame that have to be overcome, but her
    own fraught experiences with whites."—Provided by publisher.
Identifiers: LCCN 2020003064 (print) | LCCN 2020003065 (ebook) |
    ISBN 9781641602747 (cloth) | ISBN 9781641602754 (adobe pdf) |
    ISBN 9781641602761 (mobi) | ISBN 9781641602778 (epub)
Subjects: LCSH: Johnson, E. Dolores. | Jackson, Ella Lewis, 1910-2005—
    Family. | African Americans—New York—Buffalo—Biography. | African
    Americans—Race identity. | Jackson family. | Lewis family. | Racially mixed
    families—New York—Buffalo. | Interracial marriage—New York—Buffalo.
    | Indianapolis (Ind.)—Race relations. | Indianapolis (Ind.)—Biography.
Classification: LCC E185.97.J67 J64 2020 (print) | LCC E185.97.J67
    (ebook) | DDC 306.8509747/97—dc23
LC record available at https://lccn.loc.gov/2020003064
LC ebook record available at https://lccn.loc.gov/2020003065

Interior design: Nord Compo

Printed in the United States of America
5 4 3 2 1

For Mama and Jennifer, my fellow travelers

"He began to have a dim feeling that,
to attain his place in the world,
he must be himself, and not another."

—W. E. B. DuBois,
The Souls of Black Folks

"Everything can't be explained by
some general biological phrase."

—Nella Larsen, *Passing*

CONTENTS

PROLOGUE

It was sticky hot at nine o'clock that morning in Greenville, South Carolina. I was in my office, a corporate outpost in a sparsely settled section of town, sitting on a sleepy two-lane road dotted with intermittent nondescript buildings, a gas station, and thick rows of crops in patchwork fields. I readied files for customer appointments and stuffed them into my briefcase.

As I ran down the outdoor steps to the company car, the sweat on my back stuck my sheath dress to me like a bathing suit. When the car's air-conditioning kicked in, I mopped myself up with a wad of Kleenex and tried to smooth my hair, now rising like a dandelion seed head.

At the gas station across the road where the company had an account, the white gas man sauntered over. With a head bob and a grin, he started the fill-up. While pretending to wash the windshield, he stared through it instead, sizing me up, leaving water streaks across the glass.

It was the mid-1970s, when civil rights gains hadn't sunk in much in the small-town South. I had to ask myself what a black New Yorker like me was doing in that foreign land of rifle racks in pickup trucks, proudly displayed Confederate flags, and a local university that didn't let blacks set foot on campus. I was twenty-six and had moved there with my husband despite my father's warning that I didn't understand the ways of the South, the South his family had escaped in the 1930s during the Great Migration. But I was a love-struck bride, so I went anyway, thinking my husband's better job was our step up.

The gas man replaced the nozzle and came around to the driver's side. As I started the engine, ready to sign the bill, he stuck his head too close to my open window.

"You been comin' in here regular, gal," he said, his stale smoker's breath so strong I turned my head a moment. "I been a-looking at you and a-wondering, what are you anyway? You Spanish?"

"No." I refused to meet his eyes.

"Eye-talian, right? You're Eye-talian."

"No." How I hated it when people started this guessing game about which box my looks fit in.

"Injun?"

"No."

"You ain't a Jew, is you?"

"No."

"Then what? Tell me."

"Black," I said loudly to the windshield. "I'm black."

He whooped and jumped back from the car, then cupped his hands and yelled across the pumps to another attendant. "Hey Joe, come here and lookit this gal. She says she black."

Out of the corner of my eye, I saw a middle-aged white woman in an old Chevy at the next pump turn, craning to see what he was talking about.

"Get on out of that car so I can take a good look at you," he said, talking to me in a tone I imagined he saved just for blacks, demanding and superior, as though I had to obey. He reached for the driver's door handle to pull it open.

I swung my head around and faced him.

"You better step the hell out of the way if you don't want your foot run over." I hit the gas and fled the station.

But I couldn't flee the nerve he'd struck. I'd pulled up and out from my childhood ghetto, where we lived in a flat with a coal-burning stove, cringing from my black father when he raged about the racists on his job. And yet, people still challenged my identity and tried to place me outside who I knew I was. Because my light skin is beyond their binary understanding of race in the United States.

But blackness was my essence. I reveled in it; loved jive talk, grew up to diligently object to racism, from store clerks following my husband on suspicion of stealing, to corporate foot-dragging on hiring blacks. With black people—my people—I could be myself, safe from harassment or having to filter myself for white people's benefit.

There in that South Carolina gas station, I was black, according to my family, society's one-drop rule, and my government-issued birth certificate. It was culturally and legally ridiculous to wonder if I wasn't. Because the biological fact of my birth was completely beside the point and counted for nothing.

My beloved mother is white.

1

CODE SWITCH

My identity has always been tangled up in the fraught defini-
tions of America's racism, just as it was a few years later when
I drove onto the world corporate headquarters campus nestled back
in low, rolling New Jersey hills, along with thousands of other pro-
fessionals. Like them, I was suited up and carrying a presentation
for the day's meetings. Unlike the others, I was black and female.

I shut off Smokey Robinson's sweet crooning and took a minute
to shape-shift into my oh-so-heavy white mask and to rehearse the
code switching needed to get my ideas across to white colleagues.
Then I walked briskly through the maze of corridors to my office.

It was 1977. My job managing part of the national marketing
strategy for telephone companies' business communications products
was an ever-growing pile of assignments, most labeled URGENT or
VERY URGENT, all due yesterday. That meant hammering out agree-
ments with a team of engineers, lawyers, accountants, sales managers,
and factories. The work was intense, but I was up to it. The real
challenge was being respected as an equal in one of America's largest
companies, dominated by white males. Their normal old boy power
was my mountain to climb.

But I was on it, as was my husband, Luther, who had gotten a
Department of Defense job here in New Jersey after we fled that
hellacious mess down south. At least up north in New Jersey people

were more inclined to treat blacks fairly, which was some comfort. That didn't include the police, who routinely made the news profiling men stopped for driving while black. At work the company's legal compliance with affirmative action was an established procedure, though a human resources rep had called me about a form I'd turned in the first day at orientation. She had just one question, about my profile.

"Well, I mean, if it's OK, can you tell me why you checked the racial category black at the bottom?" she asked. "I have to make sure it's accurate for the Equal Employment Opportunity Commission report, is all. For the government, you know."

"You are asking what race I am, is that it?"

"That's not illegal, is it?"

I told her I marked black because I am black, and the form was correct.

"It's just when I saw you, I didn't think . . ." In a flurry of awkward thank-yous, she hung up.

At least she asked the gas attendant's "What are you?" question with some respect.

When we started working in New Jersey last year, Luther and I made up our own continuing education program at home, because doing our work and keeping our noses clean was just the ante to get jobs like ours. To earn our seat at the table, we black first-generation college grads had to polish our facades and up our gamesmanship.

We inspected each other's body language in the dining room while practicing presentations, editing out any Black English and mannerisms. During Sunday football Luther related quarterback calls and strategic blocking and tackling to being in the corporate game. "You're dealing with power players. They don't want to talk. They want to win," he said.

We made plans and contingencies for our projects and practiced speaking in headlines. As I stood in the walk-in closet in my panty hose, Luther had me recite the headlines to use at work. "Just say what the problem is and the actions you recommend for fixing it. If they want details, they'll ask. No chitchat."

I read *Dress for Success*, ditched my Sears wardrobe, and bought tailored Pendleton suits. He taught me chess, poker, and Scrabble, so I understood how to think several moves ahead, not tip my hand, and maximize every play.

We even planned how we would sort the anytime, anywhere offensive race situations into which ones we had to let go and which to take on.

For instance, at an executive meeting atop a British bank tower with the Thames River in view, the client manning the tea trolley asked the man next to me how he liked his. "White and sweet, like we like our women?" He was the customer. I couldn't call him out about race in the middle of making a deal if I wanted my job. But I did have to carry that insult back home in the pit of my stomach.

My business headshot.

There was the Atlanta company trainer who said if a customer refused to deal with my kind, even to the point of pushing me out a door as the trainer had done to me, the correct response was to go back to the office and send a white male back. I said I wouldn't; the company had to back me up.

Or another time, a Swiss colleague at an international management dinner for twenty told nigger jokes our Denver coworker taught him. I pushed away my plate and walked out. After human resources got involved, he was made to apologize.

A corporate president was taken aback at the recommendation that more minorities be hired at top levels. "But then, we'd have to have special training so they could keep up," he replied to us senior minorities on the diversity committee, oblivious that he was disparaging us to our faces.

My second job, learning to act like them and field their aggressions, though invisible to whites, was a burden I carried at the same time I did my paid job. In early days, I fought to keep my "acceptable" mask on in front of colleagues, some of whom talked over or ignored me. Later, I grew another persona, with corporate-speak rolling off my tongue, a thicker skin, and a practice of blocking and tackling people privately before my presentations so there was no ignoring me in meetings.

I thought my black executive in a white corporation card was working until a trusted black coworker called from payroll. "Hey," she said. "Is your door closed?"

"Yep." Settling in, I pulled out the bottom desk drawer and put my feet across its top, like a footstool. "What's going on?"

She had some data I might be interested in, only if I agreed she didn't tell me. The annual employee rankings for performance for my job title were in, alongside the new salaries and raises. My performance was ranked pretty high compared to my peers.

It was so great they recognized my contributions. "I'll probably get a good raise," I said.

"Well. Sort of," she said. My pay and upcoming raise were way below those white men I ranked above.

I picked at the cuticle on my left index finger. "By how much?"

"Big money." She couldn't tell me everything, but that man who took two-hour lunches with the blonde secretary was ahead of me by maybe 20 percent. The one who didn't do half the work I did. And wasn't as good.

"What I want to know," she said, "is what are you going to do about it?" There was a long pause. "I'm out, girlfriend. It's your move." She hung up.

I immediately thought about Daddy. How he put on his uniform before dawn every day and caught several buses to work, even in Buffalo blizzards. As soon as he got home, before he took his Lava soap bath, he'd drink a straight Four Roses whiskey. If his bosses had just pulled the same dirty deeds on him that mine were trying to pull now, he drank a second or third Four Roses. That, we knew, meant to watch out.

"I hate that damned job," he'd say before he sat down to eat. After grace, if he pounded the table and hollered, we knew the damned DPs, as he called the European immigrants who owned the ornamental steel company where he welded, had somehow denied the recognition, title, or pay for the work he did, because he was black or because he married a white woman. Or they had used the word *nigger*, which Daddy said was the first thing they learned when they got off the boat.

That job had turned my father into a man who balled his rage up inside in order to keep working there, then brought it home to drink and go off on us. All he knew was it took his Four Roses to deal. All I knew was to stay out of his way when he drank it, if I didn't want to somehow end up on the receiving end of his strap.

What was I going to do about my pay? Try not to turn into Daddy. It was thirty years later, and I wanted my due. Like every-body else at the office, I worked hard to move up and get paid, and I wanted to be paid fairly. If having my dream meant a continual game of whack-a-mole with white people popping up to stop my every move, I'd get my mallet out.

The day came when my boss came into my office and handed me a paper showing my raise and new salary. Had my friend not tipped me off, the amount might have looked good. But it was nowhere near that other guy's old pay, even though the boss said I was highly rated and had done great work.

I thanked him pleasantly and said it was good he appreciated my work. "But, sorry," I said, "I have to say—I'm not sure this level of pay represents what I contributed here."

It was a big risk, but one Luther and I had agreed on. If the boss got mad, it could mean trouble for me, like intentionally impossible assignments, or being transferred to a dead-end group, or out the door on some false excuse. But where was my dignity if I didn't ask for what should be mine?

My boss looked at me, his eyes dark. "It's a good salary," he said.

"But nowhere near what others in this group make; others rated lower than me, right?"

He asked me how I knew how much others made or where they were ranked.

"Because I know. Look, some people might think this discrepancy is not fair, if you know what I mean." He knew I meant discriminatory. He sat down in my visitor's chair, leaning toward me with his hands on his knees.

He asked me what I was saying.

"I want to be paid fairly, at the same level as the white men here." I leaned in too, using a poker face and speaking slowly. "And paid more than those who don't put out what I do. Can you please address this?" I had recited these exact headlines with Luther three different times in preparation for this moment.

But all the money had been distributed to employees and the payroll adjustments closed, the boss countered. The next raise would be a year from then.

I said the company could still make changes if they wanted to be equitable. "Can you see what can be done, please?" I tried not to look like that angry black woman white people are afraid of, using that layer of cultural camouflage I had learned to put on.

He nodded and went out. I tried to stop my foot patting wildly under the desk.

The next week he came in and handed me a paper stating that I was being given a significantly higher increase. Not as much as I wanted, but nothing to quibble about. I shook his hand and smiled. "Thank you very much. I appreciate what you did." After that he found a number of ways to let me know how valuable I was to the team.

That was the moment I understood there was always room to negotiate, no matter how firmly an offer is stated. Throughout my career and personal transactions, negotiation has been a useful skill, something people from humble backgrounds like mine unfortunately don't know or are afraid to try. But the price I'd paid to earn my place as a successful executive in a white corporation had worn me out. I was sick and tired of all that extra work to level the playing field. Filter. Hesitate. Pretend. Switch vocabularies. Point out inequities. Hide my pain and anger. Mask culturally natural responses. Decide which racial slight to let pass. Speak easily in well-modulated pleasantries with heedlessly entitled people.

In becoming a respected member of the team, I hadn't seen how far I'd split myself. My white-coded executive persona switched off and on like a bad romance; on with the white business world, off with black friends and family. It was exhausting. Infuriating. I was losing my center.

I had even begun to meld whiteness with my personal life before I realized it. Following an opera broadcast on TV, Luther and I wanted to hear more of the dramatic melodies of the arias. Just as we went to see Broadway musicals and pop concerts in Manhattan, Luther bought a few Thursday-night performances of live opera at the Met in Lincoln Center.

We sat up in the dress circle, the only two blacks in sight, wearing our dark suits from work. A dozen starburst crystal chandeliers rose above the red seats and into the ceiling, hushing the murmuring audience. What a spectacle the elaborate costumes and sets created on a stage that split and sunk in sections.

When two hefty lovers sang duets in notes too high and too strong to imagine, Luther leaned over. "It's my first time seeing such a big woman in a love story," he whispered. Later I learned big divas often have amazing voices.

Opera was just one way Luther and I took in white culture, stepping outside our personal all-black box. We had plenty of activities with Luther's family and members of our black church, but the older white couple next door became like family and a few colleagues became friends, sharing meals, advice, fix-its, and going to the Macy's parade before a Thanksgiving dinner.

We had a good life. While very few blacks we knew associated with whites in their private life, we became sort of integrated, moving more naturally among whites. Sort of, because integration was a teeter-totter, bouncing up with the hope that we were accepted like everybody else, then dumped down in the dirt when whites jumped off their end and challenged our right to sit on our own neighborhood beach, or ignored Luther at the paint store counter to go in the back rather than wait on him in the midst of our half-finished dining room project.

The thing was, leaning into white culture had gotten to a point where I wondered if maybe I *was* selling out. Like fitting in and enjoying the other side diluted the blackness that always defined me. I had to get out of this halfway house and get back to me. But how?

A few months later, Luther and I plopped down on our den sofa to watch *Roots*, a groundbreaking show about a black American who traced his family to the slave ancestor captured from West Africa. Soon after, magazine articles and TV interviews galore featured all kinds of Americans who searched their roots. Each one swore filling in their family tree had made them sure of who they were.

That was it. My best anchor was to learn about my family too, the southern ones Daddy and Grandma talked about but I had never met. Knowing who I came from and the history that ran through me would plant my feet back on center. Maybe if I went down and spent time with them, I wouldn't feel so lost.

2

DRESS BOX

Our relatives in Georgia and Alabama were only names and stories to me, except for Great-Aunt Willie in Birmingham. When I used to sleep over at Grandma's as a girl, she had me write letters to Willie. Daddy said Grandma went to night school for twenty years to learn to read and write, but the only thing she learned was the neighborhood gossip. Sitting at her feet, she'd pluck an unanswered letter from her wicker basket and dictate the reply to me.

"Dear Willie. Whatcha got, Dolores?"

"Dear Willie," I'd read.

"Received your letter and was glad to hear from you. Whatcha got?"

"Dear Willie, received your letter and was glad to hear from you."

"We are fine and hope you are too. Whatcha got?"

Most of the opening I'd already written before she dictated it; for years, every letter had had an identical greeting. Then we'd add the Buffalo updates and write similar content to others waiting in that basket. Our teamwork saved Grandma the extravagance of running up some long-distance phone bill she couldn't afford. And all those letters to Willie gave me a sense of kinship. With Grandma's blessing and help, I headed to Alabama.

It was no surprise the visit started with having to talk the reluctant white cabdriver in Birmingham into driving me to the black side of town. It had been fifteen years since their police dogs and maximum strength water hoses blasted demonstrating African American youth and a black Baptist church bombing killed four little girls. Maybe the driver took me because he knew I wasn't a local who would put up with his excuses, or maybe he thought I was white.

When we pulled up, Aunt Willie came down off the porch of her bungalow where she waited for me. As that stately dark woman wrapped me in a warm hug, I caught the scent of pomade in her freshly straightened hair. She was dressed for company in a wrap-around dress, and she fussed over me as only a relative with southern charm could.

"Ooooeee, look at Charles's baby come to see the old folk," she said, and laughed easily. "Come on in, chile, and rest yourself a while. You thirsty?"

We spent Friday evening talking over news of the Buffalo family she hadn't seen in decades. I delivered their messages and the recent photos they wanted her to have. She got acquainted with my mother and brothers too, none of whom she had ever seen. I, on the other hand, had to admit I didn't know about most of the people she tried to fill me in on. But I promised to take the stories back to Buffalo.

Saturday morning, Willie and I sat out on the porch with our shoes kicked off, gently swinging in her old glider. It sat under the striped awning she kept down all the time against the Alabama heat.

"I heard you went to our colored college up in Washington. Is that right?"

I began telling her about my experience at Howard University, when she stopped me.

"Oh wait, here comes Miz Greene. Mornin', Miz Greene. This is my great-niece come to visit from up north!"

"Well, I declare," Miz Greene said, asking where from, for how long, who in my way back was related to Willie. Would she know them?

By her demeanor, it wasn't clear if this conversation was courtesy or gossip fodder. I answered sweetly with just enough explanation to satisfy. "She's my daddy's aunt, from the Georgia side." After further pleasantries, Miz Greene went on her way.

Aunt Willie kept interrupting our conversation to introduce me to the whole community as they passed by, from the postman to neighbors going to and fro. Since it seemed to make Willie proud of my visit, the way she put me on display for people I didn't know, I made small talk with every person who said hey.

There was even one woman who came up on the porch to get a real good look at me. She used that southern cover-all for saying anything you want: "Bless your heart, honey." Then she asked what she really wanted to know. "But is y'all really related? You don't look nothing like Willie." That was sure the truth.

I smiled at their curious glances, feeling at once part of the community that came to greet me and an oddity in it. I wondered if Willie had told them I had a white mother, something few Americans accepted, and I doubted few southerners of either race could abide.

Out on that porch is where I found out about Daddy's first marriage. I knew he'd had a first wife, but she was never spoken of. "Weren't she purdy?" Aunt Willie asked me, assuming I already knew what she was saying about Daddy getting married at seventeen. This was fascinating, so I didn't stop her talking. But the bride I wasn't related to was not the connective family story I came to Alabama to get. When I admitted to not ever having seen her, Aunt Willie walked me back to her room where she had a picture of their wedding day to find and show me.

"Look down under the bed for me, hehe, and save these old legs," she said. "Now feel around for a dress box." It wasn't near the foot of the bed, so I scooted over to its side, lay down, and reached way underneath. There it was—a large box of sturdy cardboard. Squirming in closer to grab hold, I hooked my index finger into a pull cord that hung from inside the lid and pulled the box out. That once white box hadn't been moved in years, judging by the gray clumps of dust Willie had to wipe off with a wet rag.

"They're all in there, the family pictures," she said. "Bring the box in the dining room where we can see 'em good."

I set that heavy box on her lace tablecloth and she wiggled the lid off slowly. Inside were hundreds of black-and-white and sepia-toned pictures thrown together, jammed to the top. Some were shiny, or with scalloped white edges, or fixed to standing frames under some laminate. Every person pictured was black, very dark black. No wonder the porch people had stared so.

More of my history, identity, and roots were in that box than I'd hoped to find on this visit. And Willie was ready to help me understand what they each had to do with me.

"We have to dig through this to find that wedding picture," Willie said. "It's in there somewhere."

"Good, I want to see that, and will you also show me the other family in here I don't know?"

She started with the photos on top, a lot taken of her and her husband's occasions at church and with friends. After some stories about her life in those shots, I politely asked to just see relatives. She had no children, but for the next hour, she showed some with mostly her husband's people. I thanked her for sharing, then when I finally explained how much I wanted to understand who my own blood relatives were, Willie began sorting pictures in earnest.

In one, Grandma stood wide-legged in an overcoat, squinting into the camera on a sunny day. She was about the same age in the picture as I was at the time, around thirty.

"Ain't you the spitting image of Belia? You both got that white side, see?"

"What white side are you talking about?" I asked.

"Ain't they told you 'bout it?"

Willie said Grandma and her cousin Acie were born to the two Doster sisters that had been raped repeatedly by two white brothers. The men's family, named Riley she thought, owned the Georgia farm where the sisters worked, in Smithville. They were teenage girls in 1890 when Grandma was born, on the same farm where her ancestors had been slaves.

My great-grandmother   Aunt Acie (left) and Grandma with my brothers
Frances, who was raped.   and me. All of us were half white.

Great-aunt Acie, who I met at her place on Sugar Hill in Harlem, was pretty white looking but, like me, was unquestionably black. While the connection between her and my grandmother had never been clear to me, I'd just assumed she and Grandma were part of the chalk-to-charcoal spectrum of black people's coloring.

My throat caught as the horror sunk in. That old Massa privilege had been forced on my great-grandmother fifteen years after the Civil War? How had Grandma lived with the pain and humiliation all these years and never talked about her mother? I didn't know what to do with my outrage, sitting with the aunt who reported this as flatly as the weather forecast. That must be why Grandma called leaving Georgia "escaping."

It gave me a new pride in my grandmother, knowing she'd had the gumption to leave. She'd made a plan, probably having to sneak her family out to get away from the Smithville whites who wanted to keep their heels on her neck. I'd never known that old lady now crippled by arthritis had that kind of courage and drive. I'd never known Buffalo was her promised land.

"I guess she didn't tell me about that because she was ashamed," I said.

"'Shamed? Naw, everybody knew white men did that whenever they got ready, and there wasn't anything we could do 'bout it. In your great-grandma Frances's time, there still wasn't no getting away from those men. She was ripe, you know, sixteen or so, when she birthed Belia.'"

"Did Grandma know her father?"

The whole family knew him. Willie could still picture that white man. He'd come around once in a while with a bag of candy and set Grandma on his knee. But they all knew better than to try to claim that open secret beyond the front porch.

So that's what flowed in my veins, a white plantation rape. It was one thing to read about slavery rapes, but the subjugation of my own grandmother and her mother sickened me. Yet I would have to carry that rapist's blood with me always, not in shame but in anger. And though I didn't know it then, finding his stain wouldn't be the last time the discovery of an ancestor would change who I thought I was.

Aunt Willie went back to the box, like Grandma's story was nothing. She went on showing me other relatives whose names I'd heard but relationships I'd never grasped. As we talked, I began to lay their pictures out by sibling groups on the lace, filling half the table. I went and got a pad and pen to make notes so important details wouldn't be forgotten. When I got back to the dining room Aunt Willie had poured us her homemade sweet tea, the mark of southern hospitality. We sipped from tall glasses with lots of ice, and she pulled down the shade against the sun that had already heated up the house.

We got right back to it, the old lady as excited to tell the stories as I was to hear them. She showed me the people in Florida who sent us oranges at Christmas, people in Philadelphia, cousins I'd never met in Manhattan, people still in Georgia. Grandma's first husband, Nathan, a slight, dark railroad man who shoveled coal to fuel the engines was in a fading group picture. Willie told me he was killed on the rails in a poker fight and brought home to Grandma by his black coworkers in the back of a mule-drawn cart. Daddy hadn't told us anything about this father, either. But then Charles Nathan was obviously named for him.

I asked if she knew of any African ancestor of ours who was brought to the States. Such an identity-anchoring heritage seemed essential to me after watching *Roots*.

She nodded. The story of our African forefather had been told to her by her own parents. She said we came from a man who was brought on a slave ship to Virginia and was then sold to a Georgia plantation. Willie never knew his name. But she worked backward in time through the photo genealogy laid on that table to the timeframe when he came. We figured he was probably born about 1840, only two generations before Grandma.

Holy Moses, I am African, I thought. It felt like a lifeline from my belly had been strung through all these generations of people on the table and tied off in his. Many years later, Ancestry DNA testing would confirm his origins in Togo and Benin in West Africa. But back then, in the initial tug of my connections, I was suddenly somebody, much more than just my nuclear family, Grandma, and the Buffalo relatives. Even though I'd never meet these kinfolks, now I had generations behind me. I wrote it all down then to capture their stories.

As I did, Aunt Willie continued to dig around in that dress box. "Looky here," she said, handing me one of those laminated five-by-seven pictures. The sepia-toned photo of Daddy as a very young groom showed him to be trim and serious in a suit. I recognized him, that same strong build and wide nostrils. He stood next to a brown-skinned girl with marcel-waved hair in a drop-waist dress.

"Told you she was purty," Aunt Willie said. "Take it. You should keep the picture."

I wondered why Daddy never talked about that marriage. Was it because divorce wasn't accepted back then? And why get married at seventeen? Here were more secrets, like Grandma's white father and her husband's murder on the train. Grandma and Daddy had kept big parts of their earlier lives from us kids, as if they could erase their Georgia history.

But it wasn't erased anymore. All they lived through had become part of me. From my African beginning, through generations of plantation slavery and the rape of my formerly enslaved great-grandmother, to my father's migration out of the South, I was firmly convicted of my black roots. There were emotional ramifications to sort out, but I could go home and code switch all I wanted, as a proud black woman.

The next morning before I went home, Aunt Willie returned to the pictures we'd left on the table. "You want any more of these to keep?"

I took that one of Grandma standing wide-legged to see later if we really did favor, and a couple of recent ones of Willie to show the Buffalo family. We put the rest back in the box and I pushed it under her bed. Before getting into the black cab company's car she'd called for me, I kissed Aunt Willie and hugged her tight, wondering if she had any idea how much she'd given me.

Luther gave over the dining room to me so I could lay out the family history. A chart was typed on a legal-sized page with rows of siblings and their mates, noting marriage, birth, and death dates. When the stories were written up, the chart and Willie's photos were added and bound into books. They were ready in time to pack for our trip to Buffalo for Christmas. I couldn't wait to see my family's surprise as they unwrapped each of their own keepsake copies.

With everyone gathered for the holiday that morning, Mama's favorite cinnamon rolls, which had risen next to the heat vent overnight, were going fast. When the last bathrobe and bottle of Old Spice were opened and the wrapping paper thrown out, I said there was one more present, a special surprise. That was Luther's cue to get the family history books down from our bedroom.

"Remember when I went to see Aunt Willie last spring?" I said. "All the family history she gave me has been written down in these books. Here's a copy for each of you."

"Wow, Dolores," David said, sticking his hair pick into his out-sized Afro.

"Our African forefather is in there," I said. "Like in *Roots*."

"For real? You found our African," David said. "Too cool, my sistah."

Charles Nathan looked his over like it was an ugly Christmas tie. He was the most disengaged from the family, so I should have known he wouldn't make much of our history. Why had I thought he would care?

Daddy pulled out the genealogy chart, which was folded to fit in the 8½-by-11 binding, got out his magnifying glass, and studied the information, penciling in a few more details.

"What the hell is this?" he said, looking at the picture of himself as a seventeen-year-old groom. "I can't believe you'd show this to your mother." I said nothing, having triggered him to pour the first Four Roses of the day into his coffee and grumble about not wanting to see "that woman."

Mama said never mind, that marriage was ancient history that we kids always knew on some level. But her long-standing rule still stood: "I don't want any talk about her in my house, Dolores."

I should have thought of her feelings, and so said I was sorry. But they were missing the historical point. The picture was meant to show off our handsome young father, not his ex. We'd never seen his younger years.

David came over to where I was standing to save me. He put his arm around me. "I always wanted to know about the whole family, my beautiful black history. Thank you," he said "Now, come on, Daddy, you know we all wanted to see how dapper you were as a young lady-killer." David could say anything to Daddy because those two had a special bond. They'd been a pair of soul brothers since way back when they fell into that stupid old Amos 'n' Andy routine.

"Just tear off the ugly half of the picture if you and Mama don't want to see it," David said, and laughed as he mimicked the slow rip up the middle of a picture.

Charles Nathan hadn't said anything. As his white wife thumbed the pages, he looked on with a weak pretense of interest. Maybe he thought it was just another of my bookish tangents, a project nobody else in the family would see the point of doing. Or maybe he was quiet because he was never much of a talker.

Later, over Mama's delicious feast, Daddy had warmed up to the notion of talking about his life and started telling family stories. About his brother and wife from New York who passed through town with a woman in tow who was sawed in half in a magic act. About all the raccoon, possum, rabbit, and sparrow dinners our country relatives could fix six ways to Sunday. About how one of Grandma's white laundry customers in Smithville trained him as a gentleman's valet for her husband. That was where he learned etiquette, polite company language, professional grooming, and attire. It was delightful to laugh and learn together about the brighter sides of the father we'd seen beaten down by racism in his later years.

I was happy that Christmas because I'd made it back to center, authenticated by my multigenerational African American family. Unfortunately, that steadiness only lasted until spring.

Then I was another kind of lost.

3

LONELY ONLY

The following spring, I sat on our back deck with my genealogy chart and a cup of coffee, trying to imagine my ancestors' lives. All of them had labored at the altar of white people's profit and convenience but gained little. Generations of my enslaved ancestors had fathered generations of sharecroppers, who fathered sons who sweated in factories, and daughters who kept house (as Grandma did in a brothel) or minded white children instead of their own. According to family lore, those in my line were resilient people who loved their families, worshipped God, and made it with what little they had. It was their honesty and dignity than ran in my veins and anchored me.

Then my eyes fell further down the chart to my own parents. Why, this family search was all about Daddy's story. Only Daddy's story. In all that *Roots* searching, the one person on the whole chart who had as much to do with who I was as Daddy hadn't been considered. Mama had been taken for granted, almost invisible. She was just my mother, like anybody's mother. She cooked, cleaned, washed, and gardened, worked the night shift at the hospital, and helped us with whatever we needed. And she never made an issue of anybody's race, least of all her own. As a result, I never recognized her to be either a black mother or a white mother.

Looking out over our back lawn, I considered how Mama lived in the middle of black culture but had never really been of it. She complained that our soul music was pure noise and we complained the cascading strings on her Montovani LPs were boring. She held us to Standard English, editing out the Black English we picked up outside. "You don't 'ax' somebody, you 'ask' them," and "There's no such word as ain't." Even though David, Daddy, and I were Protestants in a black church, she also had us practice her white people's Catholicism with no-meat Fridays and candy-free Lent.

Mama was white but didn't live white. Because she was with us blacks, she was less white, a sort-of white person. She was not white like the racists Daddy railed against. But when an African American neighbor dubbed her "an honorary black woman," in a nod to her embracing-blacks sort-of whiteness, Mama pshawed the title. "It's supposed to be a compliment," she told me, "but I'm white. I have always been white, and nothing different."

But people didn't see it like that back in the 1950s. Both black and white strangers treated Mama as less than white, their chance to strip off the white privilege she'd lost by marrying black. Because we had a sort-of white mother, the whole family suffered a double-whammy prejudice, both the standard issue prejudice against blacks and the prejudice against race mixing. Out there on the back deck, I cringed, crediting Mama for the first time for shielding us kids from the intolerance, disdain, and rejection we faced in every store, bus ride, or excursion. Of course, we hadn't understood as children, but I'd recently read about a 1958 PEW Research study that found 96 percent of Americans were against race mixing. I was born ten years before that. My parents married twenty-five years before the study.

The mixed-race prejudice was in our neighborhood, at what Daddy called the black holy-roller church next door. During Sunday breakfast I strained to be heard over the pulsing beat of music urging the congregation to love God. Yet outside afterward, church members glared at our family. As a little girl I heard a woman in a lovely suit grunt like we'd done something awful by just walking by.

"Would you look at that?" she spit out to her companions.

"What's wrong, Mama?" I asked.

"Nothing's wrong," she said, walking on as if it didn't concern us.

The mixed-race prejudice was in our extended family. In those early years, Mama had no friends, so we only kept company occasionally with a few members of Daddy's people. What I'd overheard at Grandma's made me understand. She urged Mama to go with her to Uncle Butch and Edna's for meals he made from the animals he hunted or slaughtered, from raccoon and possum to the chitlins from pigs—meals Grandma loved, and Mama hated. She said they stank and weren't clean, even if Butch did put white potatoes on the lid to cut the odor.

"At least those dinners would be some company for you," Grandma said. "Ain't you lonely? Edna likes you, and Butch done got used to you."

Mama said she knew the other relatives spent time together but didn't invite us, save to an occasional birthday party with my second cousins or Christmas breakfast.

"The family's not comfortable with you, Ella," Grandma said. "I can't change that. They ain't never been around your kind."

That mixed-race prejudice was out in public everywhere we went. People on the bus stared hard at us long enough to be sure the disgust in their eyes had time to pierce. One white saleswoman waited on everyone, even those behind us, before ringing up our purchase.

Once as we rode a ferry to Crystal Beach Amusement Park on the Canadian side of Buffalo's harbor, a white mother encircled her white children and pushed them into a corner to keep them from brushing against us. All the while she glared at us, like we had cooties or something.

At a summer picnic in a county park, Charles Nathan, then ten years old and white looking, got stung by bees. He flailed his arms and rolled on the ground in a full-on meltdown while Mama tried to pull the stingers out with her fingernails. Another white woman on her way from the restrooms heard the ruckus and came over to help.

"You need mudpacks," she told Mama, stooping down to a puddle of water, mixing dirt in it to make a thick paste. When Mama packed the mud around the stingers they slid out as easily as candles from a birthday cake. She thanked the woman, who was happy to help. But when Daddy came over from the shed and hugged Charles Nathan, the woman studied first one face, then another, her smile fading.

"Won't you have some lunch?" Mama offered, motioning to the grilled food already on our table. The woman didn't seem to understand what was going on with the people she saw. Until her hand flew up to cover her mouth. I remembered how she ran away, fast, as if she was the one stung by bees.

That mixed-race prejudice came right into our living room around 1956. Mama found out she could earn twenty-five whole dollars giving room and board to some Negroes coming to a national conference in Buffalo. She could pay some bills and save at least five dollars if she handled it well. The visitors needed to stay in private homes since the white hotels and restaurants wouldn't accept them. Once listed, our flat on Hickory Street was snapped up because it sat on the direct bus line serving the conference site.

Mama scrubbed corners and washed the best sheets while Daddy shopped for good quality food for them, not the spoiled vegetables we often cut around, nor what passed for our protein, a chunk of fat back with a thin strip of lean meat we plucked hairs off before boiling it to death.

Mama and Daddy moved their clothes into the boys' closet and dresser so the visitors could use their double bed and be next to the bathroom. My brothers would sleep at Grandma's, and since I stayed home, I waited in the kitchen as instructed when the visitors arrived around dinnertime.

The skinny man in a suit shook hands with Daddy in the living room. Once sure he had the right place, the two men went outside for his wife and their suitcases. As that enormous woman in a pink feathered church hat lumbered into our living room, she told Daddy how she loved the Lord. He said we had a good Christian home.

"Hallelujah, hallelujah," she said.

Daddy set down their brown cardboard suitcase in the living room and called for Mama to come out of the kitchen. The minute she did the church woman's face creased with shock. She stepped back from Mama's outreached hand as if she'd catch leprosy.

"Who is this?" she asked Daddy.

"This is my wife, Ella."

"Your wife? This woman is your wife?" She put both fists on her hips. "Somebody shoulda tolt us 'bout this," she barked, shaking her head back and forth hard enough to twist it off.

"Now hold on, Miss," Daddy said, stepping in front of Mama. "Hold on. My wife's a good lady and she worked hard to fix up nice for you here."

"Oh no," the woman told her husband. "We ain't staying here with this white woman."

She turned to him, pointed at the suitcase, and headed to the door. "Come on here," she said. "We ain't ruining our vacation lookin' at this nigger and his white trash cracker all week." The husband hurried out into the heat of the summer afternoon behind his wife, who was already across our cement patch and headed toward the alley.

"Some Christians you are," Daddy called down our alleyway. "Equal opportunity prejudice at work," he said to Mama. "Black people trying to out-hate white ones." He got out the bottle of Four Roses he'd hidden from them and poured both himself and Mama a drink. I'd never seen Mama drink whiskey, but she reached for the pink plastic cup and took a swallow right away. I was sent down the block to bring Grandma and the boys back.

Grandma, who everybody was scared of, stormed down the block, my brothers trailing behind. Her thin house dress was hitched up six inches higher in the back than the front because of her considerable backside, her lips were poked out, and her plaited hair flopped in time to her hurried steps. We also knew to stay out of Grandma's way when she got mad. Her temper was every bit as bad as Daddy's, with no liquor needed to ignite it. When she burst through our door, I stood way back.

"You should've called me," she told Daddy, her age-spotted hand jerking up over her head like a band leader. "I'd a slapped her silly."

"I know you would, Mom." Daddy shook his head and took another swallow of Four Roses. I waited in my corner for his outburst, but he did not holler. Instead his voice was firm and steady. "Nobody else we don't know and can't trust is coming in our house again. Never."

The calm in his voice said this would be law.

Mama spread the table with the hot fried chicken and mashed potatoes prepared for the conventioneers. Before eating, Daddy lifted his glass.

"To hell with that heifer and her weasel husband."

"Fuck 'em," Grandma said, intently scooping up her potatoes.

The weight of all those abusive memories had me slumped over the picnic table on my back deck. Considering the whole of them now, without the hard-shell you-can't-hurt-me façade I put on for current-day perpetrators, the quicksand of low self-esteem and of not belonging that had pulled at all my family could not be denied.

But there was more. Maybe the worst of the mixed-race prejudice was that cloudless afternoon when my Sunday-sharp Daddy put on his wide-brimmed hat and said he had a big surprise for us. We followed him out of the alley from our flat to the street, where he opened the passenger door to a green 1940-something secondhand sedan. With an amused bow to Mama, he helped her into our first car, while we three kids shrieked in excitement and jumped in back. I felt as grand as a TV star as we started off on what Mama called a leisurely ride. Daddy drove beyond downtown and up onto a bridge in a part of town I'd never been to. Smiling over his shoulder, he said we'd see a part of the bridge he built, some work he did on his job.

"Where, Daddy? What part did you make?" David asked.

He slowed way down at the center of the bridge, pointing out seams in the gray metal where he'd welded parts together with a blow torch. As he continued past it, we kept looking out the back window, imprinting the amazement of Daddy's own bridge. A bridge he said wouldn't fall, no matter how many cars and trucks were on it.

In a low voice, Daddy told Mama to look left, at the police car driving up alongside. Two white officers leaned over, eyeing both my parents menacingly. Daddy stopped at the red light at the foot of the bridge, just as their blue lights began flashing.

"Please, Charles, don't say anything," Mama pleaded, patting his leg. "Don't argue with them." Daddy shifted his weight and sat up straight. A policeman built like a wrestler in the arena shows we went to came to Daddy's window.

"What do we have here?" he said. "A nigger and a white woman. With their three little mongrels in the back. Speeding, too."

When he went to write down our license plate number, Mama warned Daddy again. "Put your hands down where he can see them and don't talk back. Please."

The officer shoved a ticket through the window at Daddy. "Go back where you came from, nigger, and don't you dare be caught driving over here again, where you don't belong. I'll be watching for you, and this woman."

I wanted so badly for Daddy to explain. To tell the policeman we were looking at his bridge. But he didn't. The father who always lectured and shouted at us, that we were afraid would spank us, sat mute and stared into his lap. Both officers stood in the street considering him, like a dare. One spit on the ground by our car before they went back to the squad car, lights still flashing. Daddy started our engine and made a U-turn, heading back over the bridge at a crawl, while the police stood by their car and watched us with revulsion.

Once back over the bridge and out of earshot, Daddy exploded. "Sons-a-bitches," he roared. "Motherfucking rotten sons-a-bitches." Seeing his face turned as hard as those steel beams he'd made, we children cowered in the back seat and kept our mouths shut.

"OK, Charles," Mama said. "We'll pay the fine and you can go home in one piece. They might've beaten you up or taken you in if you gave them any reason. You did the right thing."

I lay down on my deck bench, crying. The police had rendered my powerful father a timid subservient in front of us, because he had a white woman. They disrespected Mama for having a black man, skipping any normal courtesies given white women. Because she was only a sort-of white woman.

Oh, but I was grateful Mama had not belabored those prejudices in my impressionable years. She carried herself as a decent person and helped us see ourselves the same way, despite how others acted toward us. We

The Jackson family in the 1950s. Front (left to right): David, Dolores, Charles Nathan. Back row: Charles and Ella.

never had the woe-is-me talk about mixed-race prejudice. Instead, she modeled how to let such "foolishness" roll off our backs as best we could.

———————

I came in from the deck to the kitchen and put some chicken on to boil, making a stock for soup. There had to be something to show for my morning when Luther came back from his tennis game. As I chopped carrots, onions, and celery for the broth, I thought of how Mama gave us something perhaps even more valuable, an environment where we could live free of those prejudices, accepted and loved just as we were.

When it was time for my oldest brother, Charles Nathan, to go to school, Mama enrolled him in the neighborhood Catholic school, St. Columbus, to give him the same education and religion she had as a girl. On the first day, she was amazed to see another white woman with a caramel-colored little girl. She had never met another white woman in a mixed marriage, and she wanted desperately to meet this one. Mama caught her eye and smiled intentionally. The woman smiled back brightly and moved across the room to say hello. Marie was a vivacious pixie with a mane of curly dark hair, who commented knowingly that their children had something in common. As the nun settled the children into class, Mama and Marie stepped outside and kept talking. Marie grew up in Buffalo and was part of a big community. And she lived so close, only ten minutes away.

"Come on over to my place for coffee some morning after the kids are in school," Marie said.

"Love to," Mama said. "Thank you so much." It was the end of her drought, her first Buffalo invitation outside of Daddy's family. An invitation from not just any woman, but a woman who, like herself, married a black man. It would finally be her chance to have a girlfriend of her own, someone who also lived the mixed-race life.

Marie said if it was OK, she had two other close friends to invite to coffee with them. Angela and Sally were other white women in mixed marriages with kids at St. Columbus too.

"Can't wait to meet them," Mama said.

At Marie's, the three women greeted her warmly. Sally, dressed to the nines, was of Sicilian descent and olive complexioned, something like a light-skinned Negro. Angela, who seemed the heart of the group, had eyes that had seen it all. The coffee was ready, so they filled their cups and gathered around the kitchen table to introduce themselves.

"Where have you been hiding?" Marie asked, surprised Mama had lived just a few blocks away for six or seven years and they hadn't met. "After all, we do stick out."

Marie's mother, an Italian immigrant who lived in the flat downstairs, came up with a plate of homemade pizelles and said a brief hello in Italish. Marie and Sally had grown up together in Buffalo's Little Italy, and they'd known Angela a long time. They were as familiar as family and they included Mama like she was one of them. They had so much in common to talk about—black husbands, children of similar ages, favorite soap operas, their Catholic parish, and the neighborhood.

When it was time to go, Angela told Mama they had a larger circle of friends she should meet. Many of them were in show business, as were Marie, a cabaret singer, and both Marie's and Angela's husbands, who played in a jazz band together.

"Our friends stick together. We help each other and make our own fun in the privacy of our own homes," Angela said. "There's couples and kids, singles, blacks and whites; all kinds. We're people like you, who don't give a diddly squat about race."

That band of maybe thirty people became more than our family. They were the affirming community who made our mixed-race lives normal. The kids were our constant playmates turned cousins, the women like Mama's sisters, and the men hardworking friends. There were birthday parties and holidays, white first communion dresses, dance recitals, picnics, and all the belly laughs Mama needed when those women got to wisecracking on nuns and bosses. In time, the ladies formalized that cocoon, naming themselves the Clique Club, and setting out a full calendar of activities.

The thing I loved best about the Clique Club was the annual summer picnic at Chestnut Ridge Park, when we escaped the city cement to run free in fresh air. Out there were the just-me-and-Mama moments when we'd cuddle up on a bench and she'd teach me to appreciate nature. She pointed out how clouds floated by in an open sky and the wind sang through the pines that we never noticed in the city. I remember her closing her eyes in that park to listen to the birds and dreaming aloud of moving one day to a neighborhood where we could see beauty like that anytime.

In the park's biggest shed, which was reserved well in advance, were ample tables under the roof, alongside grills, playground equipment, and enough open space for the whole group and many other friends to get loose.

In that secluded place, our bunch of kids in every skin shade could play together outside without the usual public judgement. We always had a hike led by the oldest boys; we ran off into the woods, climbing over fallen logs in ravines, shouting echoes in the forest, and getting filthy catching frogs and bugs to take home in jars.

Our black fathers could finally relax out there. Somebody would bring horseshoes and prepare the pits, where a bunch of men would strip to their undershirts and trash talk every pitch. Others played marathon poker, all of them drinking their favorites "tastes."

The black radio station played in the background and the sepia swing revue dancers from Buffalo's Club Moonglo, the western New York hotspot where some of the fathers played jazz, showed new dance moves, everybody snapping their fingers and hooting.

Out there the affection between black men and white women was open and natural, sweet and beautiful. That rarely seen thing was captured in a 1952 photo I still have. George Williams wore a broad-brimmed straw hat over his dark face. He sat wide legged on the back fender of his 1940s sedan hugging his alabaster Angela. She wore shorts and a halter top and had one arm around his shoulders, the other on his chest; his arm hugged her right hip. Our cloistered world out in the woods made this kind of love instinctive, even as it was a love America could not imagine for another fifteen years, when mixed-race marriage would become legal everywhere.

The thing Mama loved best about the Clique Club was when her friends got together monthly for Pokeno parties. I remembered a night when Mama hosted, back when I was about eleven. Several ladies piled through the door, including Sally, Marie, and Angela. By then, Angela was the one who called most often and had lots of play dates for her daughter Sandra and me while she and Mama visited.

"Hey, you baby cakes, we're gonna have some fun tonight," Sally said.

I'd planted myself at the top of the stairs out of sight, where I could hear everything. Part of the cousins' pact was to report back from the parties what we were getting for Christmas and what the parents were fighting about.

Mama's buttery pineapple upside-down cake and dainty flowered coffee cups sat next to a new bottle of Mogan David wine waiting on the dining room sideboard. They caught up a bit, laughing at their stories a while, then passed out the Pokeno boards and started calling cards. I half listened, reading *Reader's Digest* on the steps while waiting for something interesting to happen.

"There's more money in this pot than you can make on a busy corner Saturday night, *capisce?*" Sally said, winning the final pot in their game. The bowlful of coins clinked as they tumbled out on top of each other and she scooped them up.

Later, the dessert was served, and the juicy talk I waited for started. First was the show business talk. Count Basie was coming to the Black Musicians' Club to jam before a big appearance in Buffalo. Betty James

Clique Club girlfriends at the Moonglo nightclub. Mama is third from left. One face obscured by request.

would be dancing in the new Moonglo floor show, which meant nothing to me at the time. Decades later, I realized that was where her son, Rick James, the Grammy-winning "Super Freak" funk master, got his chops.

Marie said her parents were keeping Diane at their place most of the time, getting her to and from school. It helped, so she and Bill could do more shows; her singing soft jazz at white clubs on one side of town and him leading the band at the black Club Moonglo on the other. The problem was, while Diane was with her white grandparents they tried to make the girl believe she was Italian, not black. They were proud of the old country and said it hurt their feelings that Diane didn't claim it.

"Diane asked me which side was better," Marie said, "her Italian side or her black side. I told her no side was better, but in America, half black may as well be full black."

"You got that right," Sally said.

Diane had always been black just like the rest of us. And now she wasn't? How could a black girl be an Italian girl? I felt sorry for Diane, glad I didn't have to worry about taking sides. We didn't have any other side in my house.

But the thing that really got me was when Angela said she was going out of state to Smalltown to visit her other family. It had been a couple of months since she was home.

What? What other family was she talking about, I wondered.

Sally offered to see about the kids while she was gone, but Angela said that wasn't necessary, that the kids could take care of themselves. Her oldest was a teenager who would be in charge. She'd leave them sandwiches and cereal and be back Sunday night. George would be in and out because he was working hard on new trumpet riffs.

Angela made that scenario seem like it was normal, but I knew Mama would never leave us like that. Who would help Sandra fix her thick, hard-to-comb hair? And what about hot dinners?

Marie told Angela she'd never understood how Angela's white family in Smalltown hadn't known about her black Buffalo family all these years. How had she gone to all those birthday parties, showers, even holidays for almost twenty years and still kept them from knowing she had a black husband and three black kids? Either they were the dumbest damned people, or they had an idea about her double life and didn't want to face it.

The room went quiet.

"I've told them so many lies for so many years," Angela said. "That's how come they don't know." For such an opinionated woman, this once Angela sounded as numb as a victim standing by the smoldering ruins of her house fire. "That tale I keep feeding them about me being a single career woman is such a spaghetti tangle I couldn't undo it if my parents suddenly forgot to be racists. The lie is to protect George, you know. They'd kill him if they knew we were together, just like they said way back when they had our marriage annulled and ran him out of town."

Run out of town? Like with threats and guns? And what did annul mean?

Sally asked Angela why in the world she kept going back to them then.

"I'll never give them up. I've got to have my Buffalo family and my Smalltown family." Angela went on about how much fun they had at the Smalltown family parties and holidays, how they laughed their heads off the whole time with their jokes.

"They told nigger jokes," Sally told me years later, although Angela's daughter doesn't remember hearing anything about that.

In those days, black people told nigger jokes all the time. But white people weren't supposed to. Back then in the 1950s, black people like Daddy and Grandma, neighbors, people in the supermarket or barbershop, David's friends called each other nigger. My nigger! Nigger, please. See those niggers over there? How's a nigger like you going to get a girl like that? He's the HNIC (head nigger in charge). You niggers want to come over and play some records? You little niggers line up if you want to see Santa. Nigger, nigger, nigger was just like saying "Hey man." But if a white person said it, we knew it was a slur. So why wouldn't Angela tell her white relatives to stop? How could somebody who welcomed all kinds of black people in her house, and loved her three brown children as much as any mother did, put up with that?

Later that night I woke up when the house was quiet and dark, troubled. I went to my parents' bedroom door and knocked until a light came on and Daddy opened the door.

"What's the matter?" he said.

"I want to talk," I said.

He let me in and got back under the covers, patting the bed for me to sit down.

"Why does Angela keep her kids and husband a secret from her other family?" I asked.

Mama cleared her throat. Daddy held his palm up at me like a traffic cop.

"Listen, now," he said. "This is grown-folks' business."

I went on anyway, because I'd tried but could not understand why she would pretend to anybody that my "cousin" Sandra wasn't her daughter. She was her mother. And then deny her husband too?

"I want to know," I said, "if you pretend we're not your kids too? Trick people about me and David and Charles Nathan, like we don't belong to you?"

"Dolores, you woke us up to ask a fool thing like that?" Daddy said. "You're our kids and everybody knows it. What Angela does is her business, and I don't want you to ask any more about it."

It was only on that spring day, as my adult-self dumped vegetables and seasonings in with the boiled chicken in my stock pot that I saw how our Clique Club cocoon had bred its own mixed-race confusion. The club could not make it safe out in the real world, not even among our extended families, black or white. I didn't understand it back then but being in a mixed community meant living in a world of secrets, lies, and rejections. Once the party hats and Pokeno boards were put away, the gashes left by our mothers' sort-of whiteness and our black fathers' defenses of their wives to their own black families festered. Those white women had subordinated their own cultures, acquiescing to the blackness of their husbands. I realized all the white women in the club had troubled relationships with their white families. Except Mama. Because her white family didn't exist.

It seemed ridiculous then. We Jackson children internalized the erasure of her unspoken background from the beginning. We lived without ever asking or saying anything about her white family and had zero knowledge of or interaction with Mama's family. I grabbed that genealogy chart off the back deck and saw she was the lonely, only white person on that filled-up legal-sized paper. Suddenly, her being alone, all by her white self in this black family was shocking.

"My God," I cried. Her whole white family was missing. She didn't have a single branch on that tree of her own. For the first time I realized she was my whole white family all by herself. Who Mama was had never once been questioned. What happened to *her* people, and why hadn't I ever heard about or seen them? It didn't make a scintilla of sense, my never once thinking she must have white relatives. I was an idiot.

A fuzzy memory came back to me from when I was a little girl. Our family was walking down Hickory Street going to Fred Perry's ice cream shop. The boys led the way, talking about the flavors they might get, while I walked between Daddy and Mama.

"Look at old man Henry Lewis walking," Daddy said, pointing at the way David walked. Mama laughed and nodded in agreement.

"Who's Henry Lewis?" I asked.

"He was your mother's father," Daddy said. "But never mind that." I think that's what he said, but he sent me ahead to tell Grandma to come get a treat with us. While I ran the half block to knock on Grandma's door, Mama's father had melted away and was gone, like ice cream on my tongue. My Mama had come from some family.

Then who did that make us Jacksons? Black, white, sort-of white, sort-of black? We'd been in a racial petri dish all along, shape-shifting across membranes without acknowledging it. Charles Nathan wasn't exactly white passing, though he didn't volunteer his blackness often, while David decided to be blacker than Daddy. Mama was sort-of white and here I was, wobbling worse than ever, first black, then leaning too close to white corporate America, then anchored in slave ancestors, and now captive to a phantom white family.

Luther drove into the garage and came slowly up to the kitchen, clearly having overdone it again. He poured a tall glass of ice water, pulled off his tennis whites, and got in the shower. I hid my family chart under my place setting, hardly able to wait for him to come to the table. When he did, I spooned up the soup and spread the genealogy chart across his bowl.

"My mother's family is missing," I said, pointing to her box. "There are no more white people on here. No parents. No grandparents. See, no white family. Where is my white family?"

He looked at me expectantly.

"I have a whole white half, but Mama raised me to be all black. Of course, there is no acceptance in America to be equally white and black, but *I* want to know what it means to *me*, if anything. Because now I'm not sure what that means or who I am."

"Oh my Lord," he said. "Again?"

"How can anybody know who they are without understanding both their mother's and father's background? I need to know about all of the people in me, just like you know the hundreds of people in your North Carolina roots."

His eyelashes fluttered in exasperation. "I'm too tired now to deal with this. But let me say, if your mother has a family and hasn't told you about them, there's a reason. If you want to know about them, you're going to have to ask her. My question is whether this so-called 'knowing who you are' will be worth the trouble it's going to start."

His warning didn't change my mind. I had a right to know about my family. Maybe they were all dead from some accident. Maybe they'd been against her marrying Daddy. That would be painful for Mama to tell me, but she and Daddy had been married thirty-six years. With that much time gone by, did it matter now?

If her dad's name was Henry Lewis, that would make Mama a Lewis too. Merna Elizabeth Lewis. I checked but found no trace of them in Buffalo. I didn't know where to look for her vanished people, any more than I could locate evaporating steam. Back then, in 1979, I was in pre-Internet, pre-Ancestry.com days, so I studied up on the best sources to find "lost" family and got some ideas of what facts would help. I needed a plan to get the information out of Mama for me to find out who I was.

I wasn't going to pussyfoot about it either.

4

MY WHOLE SELF

A fluffy snow fell that Friday night as I slid into a seat at our old Formica kitchen table. I took my place between my militant brother David in his dashiki and Afro the size of a pumpkin and my sometimes suspected of white-passing brother Charles Nathan, with his straight hair and granite eyes. My elderly little white mother and black father, now subdued by his pacemaker, gladly presided over a favorite meatloaf meal, pleased to have all their grown children back under one roof. They all thought I was back in Buffalo just for a visit, not suspecting I had an agenda.

When I took the conversation away from the Buffalo Bills and said I had something important on my heart to talk to them about, Mama gave me a curious smile.

I mentioned the family history books they received at Christmas and said how comforting it was they had supported my *Roots* project and my motivation to get regrounded in the black identity that sustained me. David gave me his usual side eye, signaling everyone hadn't cared like I did.

Now, I told them, there was something else. Something bigger.

We still didn't know who we were because a big piece of our history was missing. Daddy looked up, puzzled. I couldn't see Mama's face the way she was bent over to slice more meat.

"What's missing?" David said.

I got up and put my arm around Mama's shoulders and saw she didn't understand where this was going.

"Mama's side of the family is missing. Our entire white family is missing."

Mama jerked her head back and pulled away from me with the little power of the hunched-over lady she was. Her forehead creased deeply with worry grooves. This was going to be as messy as Luther predicted when he begged off coming.

Dishes and silverware clattered. Everybody stopped eating to look at me like I didn't have good sense. Mama pushed up so straight in her chair, her rarely seen knees were exposed under her house dress.

"What do you mean?" she said.

"Growing up, it never mattered we didn't know about your people," I said. "I didn't think about it, or even care, just like you didn't care."

"I didn't care? The I-dea. The very I-dea." That was as close to cussing as Mama came. "You don't know what you're talking about."

"Mama, I'm sorry. But I'm having a big problem here, trying to figure out who I am. All of me, including my white side. You never told us about your family, like they didn't exist. It's making me crazy, like the black person I always knew I was isn't my whole self. I can't live with that."

Daddy snapped his suspenders and shouted, "Aw, shit." Thankfully he hadn't had too much to drink yet, and his unfiltered temper was still at bay. I held my ground in silence, watching them watch me. David rolled his eyes knowingly at Daddy. There she goes again, the gesture said. Off on another of her tangents.

"You want to know what I've never told you?" Mama said. "Don't you understand I didn't want to talk about it?" she said, her voice rising. "Why are you doing this? What for?"

"So I can get a whole sense of myself. I want to know what that whiteness means in me. Is there something in my blank half that will mean something to who I am? Until I know about the blood running through me, I can't rest. I don't want to hurt or upset you."

She looked frail then, a sixty-nine-year-old retiree, afraid of ghosts.

"My identity is always being poked at," I went on. "As if my looks make my life out of order. People look at me like I'm some kind of freak. A white coworker asked why I'd call myself black when I could pass for white. A black one told me I wasn't better than him just because I was light. I'm tired of it."

Charles Nathan laid his napkin on the plate and shoved it away. "Uh-huh," he said. "Like that boy that busted my head open on Hickory Street when I was ten."

He'd been crawling around in the vacant lot at the end of the block looking for pennies. Some boy picked up a length of wood with a nail sticking out and slammed it into my brother's head, sending him to the hospital for stitches. The boy said he did it because Charles Nathan looked white.

Mama's eyelids drooped wearily. "I know."

"I guess you want to secede from the race now," David blared. He hammered his thumb back over his shoulder, an umpire calling me out.

"Stop it," I said. "It scares me that black people could think I'm disloyal or a misguided fool talking about my white blood. It's always been Afrocentric everything for me, and I don't want to risk not fitting in where I've always belonged. But I didn't expect you to be the first one to start this."

"Oh yeah, people are gonna talk bad about you," he said. "Guaran-damned-teed."

"Don't you get it, man? There's no permission in America to be half white. But we are! And I won't be satisfied until I know what half white means—for me." I turned to my mother, the only one whose agreement mattered. "Will you help me? Please?"

She looked at Daddy questioningly. After a very pregnant moment, he took her upstairs to talk. We were to clean up the kitchen like we did as kids and wait until they came back.

We heard their murmuring voices in the bedroom above us. Daddy's rose and fell; Mama cried and cried. I couldn't tell what they said over David's jabbering about how he didn't need to know about Mama's white people.

"I've kinda wondered too," Charles Nathan said, grabbing a dish towel. "Not about Mama's family, but what it would have been like to have two parents the same race. My life would have been so much simpler."

He'd grown up being excluded or ejected from black parties because he looked too white. Black boys spilled out of a dance and into the street to run him off the last time he tried to go where he'd been invited. What really set him apart was his lack of street culture. David and I honed our bravado on the tough-talking public school playgrounds.

Our light skin seemed irrelevant because we were street-smart, slang-talking, Motown-dancing machines that would crack on you to shut you up. But Charles Nathan was a quiet Catholic school kid who didn't know the neighborhood crowd well, couldn't dance, and wouldn't tell people where to get off. But his leaning into the white world hadn't been easy either.

When he decided to marry his white wife, Gee, in the early 1970s, his new in-laws were so upset that he was "part black," they decided on a small family wedding and private dinner instead of a larger affair. David, offended at the notion that our wider black circle wouldn't be included, complained at home, but he stood in as best man for his brother's sake. With all that drama in play, I begged off attending, using the excuse that I couldn't get back to Buffalo because of grad school commitments.

David and I left Charles Nathan to his own version of limbo, a whiteish man who lived on the white side of town with his white wife and friends. Our family still had Christmas together, and I later learned that Charles Nathan played cards with black family members during the years I didn't live in Buffalo. However much passing he did elsewhere, if it's fair to call it that, we were still connected. His blond kids identified as "part black" and, like Charles Nathan, took white partners.

As we did the dishes and waited for our parents to come back downstairs, Charles Nathan told me, "I get what you mean, about not knowing who you are, Dolores." He set the plate he was drying down. "People won't take me for who I am either. It's made me a loner, so I stick to the few people who accept me." He and his wife, Gee, dressed alike in loose shirttails, nodded at each other.

David got out the bourbon and poured himself one, then motioned the tip of the bottle toward us.

"I definitely need one," I said, holding out one of the pink cups Daddy drank his bourbon from for as long as I could remember.

"The price of you trying to be cute," he said.

It was nearly an hour later when our parents came down. They stood side by side in the living room. Stiff, like for some official hearing.

Mama raised her chin defiantly. "I left my family," she announced "I didn't mean for them to ever find me. And they never have, in over thirty-five years. And you, Dolores, are not to interfere with that."

"You left them?" I said. "But why?"

"For your father. I ran away with your father." She pulled the Kleenex from her sleeve and wiped her nose. "You kids have no idea what went on in 1943 when we decided to marry. Why, mixed marriage was *unthinkable* then. The whole country was against it."

"We couldn't stay where we were in Indiana," Daddy said. "It was as dangerous to be together there as it would have been down south. And just as illegal for us to get married."

"Dangerous? What kind of dangerous?" I asked.

"We didn't want you kids to know we could have gone to prison for being together," Mama said, coming over to sit down next to me. "We were afraid Daddy would get hurt, so we left." They decided before we were born not to scare us with the ugly truth, not to raise us knowing that kind of fear and hate.

Daddy said they had given us a family—a black family and raised us black because that was the only choice there was. "You sure couldn't have your white family in the 1940s. We did what we had to do. Now here you come wanting to change everything. After all we went through."

"But in all this time, you have never told us what you went through," I said. "Our full story has been kept from us all these years and here we are adults. But now, I just want to find out about my white side, like how I traced your family back to the African. I've even been thinking about going to look for our white family."

The sound Mama made was like wind forcing through a door crack. "OK, Daddy and I have agreed to tell you some things about my family. But if that's not enough to suit you, if you would go so far as to go find my family—" she said softly, "Why, I could never face them again, not after disappearing without a word." Her lips quivered. "They would hate me for what I did."

"You didn't tell them you were leaving, Mama? You just left?" I said.

"They don't know I'm alive," she said, looking me straight in the eye. My own plain-living mother was a runaway, hiding like some underground criminal.

"Your family thinks you're dead?" David said.

"They loved me back then, but now? I couldn't stand it, seeing them turn on me." She said that part of her life had been done with for so long, it would kill her.

"I would never let them hurt you, Mama, even if they tried. Tell us, what did they do to you and Daddy?"

"Nothing," Mama said. "They never knew about Daddy."

Could I go ahead with my plan and risk all she'd hidden for so long? Or should I drop what I wanted most, what I'd prepared for, what I needed to settle down?

I just couldn't give up and accept a life of confusion.

"I'm sorry you had to lose your family, Mama, and sorry you had to face that all over again today," I said. "But what if I could come up with a way for me to find out enough about the white family that would clear up who I was and still protect your secret?"

I asked the boys what they thought about me going out to Indiana.

Charles Nathan hunched his shoulders. "It's up to Mama."

"And you, David?"

"You already know who you are, Sapphire," he said, calling me the battle-axe on *Amos 'n' Andy*. "A pure black woman since the day you were born. After all this fighting The Man for our rights, I ain't got no questions about who I am." He pulled out the white handkerchief he always carried, swabbing his brow. David sweated even when he wasn't doing anything.

"I don't have any questions," Mama corrected him.

"I don't have any questions," David recited. "But Dolores, what are you going to get out of finding those so-called white relatives you want to meet so bad? If they wouldn't accept Daddy, don't you know they're going to slam the door in your face?"

"How do you know what they're going to do?"

He left leaning against the door frame to get in my face. "'Cause the last thing those people want to know is that their daughter married a black man, and now they got a nigger relative on the porch."

I didn't care what David said. I could take it and was willing to risk whatever they dished out. All I wanted was to see what they looked like, what type of place they lived in, and get some sense of the stock running through me. If they ordered me off their property, then I'd be able to forget this whole white blood business. I could turn my back on them too, like Mama did, and go on being my black self. If they acted like that, all my questions would be answered. I wouldn't want any of them in me.

"Your mother means we broke the law," Daddy said, trying to make us understand there could be jail time if the authorities came after him or even Mama like they could have done in the 1940s. "I'm not busting any rocks for this stuff you're talking about."

"Nobody's going to jail in 1979 for something you did forty years ago," I said.

Daddy held up his finger. "Racism is still alive and well in America, girl. You just remember that, and don't bring no trouble to your mother and me. You hear?"

"Yes, Daddy. But Mama, are your family racists? Will they shut the door on me?"

"They're simple, decent people, but they wouldn't have accepted our marriage. It would have devastated them to know what I did."

"How about this," I said. "I go to Indianapolis by myself to find out about your mom and dad. I get to see who they are and nobody in Buffalo has to face them or get in trouble. Is that OK, Mama?"

She didn't answer.

"Listen here," David said. "You better not mess this up. You do, and I'm gonna put a hurt on you." He was all bluster whenever his dander was up, so I knew not to get in it with him. Instead, I turned back to Mama.

"If I found anybody in your family who'd talk to me, Mama, what do you want me to say about you, to protect you. Just tell me what you want me to do and I'll do it. Then we both get what we need."

She wrung her wrinkled hands together, as she always did when things got out of control, her distended blue veins rolling back and forth across their backs. It seemed she would speak several times, but then she sighed and wrestled with herself some more.

"I'm so ashamed. After the way they loved me." Tears dripped down her cheeks as she rubbed the loose skin around her eyes. "But I still think what your father and I did was right. I won't have any part in this, Dolores. You want to do this for yourself, and I understand that, to a point. But please, do you promise to leave me out of it entirely?"

"OK, yes, Mama. I promise. But what am I supposed to tell them about you?"

"You'll have to . . ." She put her hand on her cheek, where her pinky finger shook. "You'll have to say . . . say I'm . . . dead."

5

DETAILS

That night, I lay in the twin bed still in my tiny pink bedroom, relieved my parents had agreed to sleep on my idea.

If only Mama would come around like she had when I'd struck out on new paths nobody understood before. Like when I left Buffalo and blue-collar life to go to college and the executive suite, Mama was the one who got behind those opportunities. Unlike David, who accused me of thinking I was better than the rest of them. Like when her nurses' aide-self called the head of the Sloan Foundation out of a meeting to get my graduate fellowship transferred to Harvard when the funds had already gone to Colombia, my second choice.

"Everything's straightened out," she told me. "The man said you are to go to Harvard."

"What man?" I said.

"The top man on the brochure." Mama had no idea she'd dealt with an executive, nor what a breach in business protocol her interruption was. She had fixed it for her baby. That was her, my constant cheerleader, even when she didn't know quite what we were cheering for.

My dreams, counter to family expectations, began in adolescence, during Saturday housecleaning. I told her I wasn't going to clean my own house as an adult, because I'd have a cleaning woman. She threw her head back and laughed, then put the dust rag and furniture polish

45

in my hands. "Until then," she said, "get to work." Years later, when she met my cleaning lady, she gave me a wry smile and threw her head back to laugh the same way.

The time she asked to see my corporate workplace in New Jersey, I took her to the sprawling headquarters campus on the weekend when nobody was around. Mama walked wide-eyed into my office, asking if it was really mine, even though she saw my name on the door.

"How much money do you make?" she asked.

I told her.

"Dolores, what can you do that would be worth that much?"

I gave her a short explanation about marketing tech products.

"I don't know where you came from, or even what you mean," she said, sitting in the leather chair behind my desk in that tan car coat she'd worn forever. "But more power to you."

Our umbilical cord was still attached that way. Always would be. And that's what I banked on to get her consent for our white family search.

I turned around in the narrow bed, putting my face at its foot, and cracked the window to feel the cool breeze on my cheeks. The soothing old sound of branches crackling on our backyard tree had always helped me think straight. And then I saw it, how selfish my need to see the white family was when it would upend Mama's painfully constructed secret. As the breeze wafted over me, I resolved to find a way that she would not get hurt if I moved forward. A way that would keep what she'd shown that evening off her face, the same deep-seated fear she'd shown when David got drafted and shipped out to Vietnam at nineteen.

She'd transferred on I don't know how many Greyhound buses across the country to see him off to Asia from his army base. Then every day he was gone, she watched Walter Cronkite's six o'clock news, or read war accounts in the morning *Courier Express*. In a small notebook on the hall table, she wrote down reported infantry units' movements and the count of American dead for all thirteen months he was at war. She and Daddy sat at the kitchen table studying that notebook, their ashtray full of the Viceroy filters she'd taken up and his ever-present Camels, praying together for their son.

David did come home, to the painted WELCOME HOME sheet hanging from the second-floor window of our house. He was fit and deeply tanned, but he was not fine. His deadly combat experiences marked him with the post-traumatic stress disorder that left him unpredictable and screaming in the night. The Agent Orange he'd been sprayed with in the jungles produced abnormal growths the size of grapefruit on his jaw and in his stomach and intestines. It left our handsome and vibrant David afraid to ever risk having children for fear of them being deformed.

He also came back from the war wedded to the black power movement. David was radicalized by the multitude of black foot soldiers he fought alongside of, used as cannon fodder in a white man's war that none of them understood. He'd seen too many be the point man of a triangular search formation, the position where his best buddy was blown into unrecognizable pieces when he stepped on a landmine. David railed against the honkies in Washington that used them to kill foreigners, ruining their lives, then treating them like no-'count niggers back in the States. All that race talk made Mama so afraid, she tearfully asked David if he counted her among the white devils.

"Not you, Mama." David assured her. "Of course, not you," he said, petting her tenderly until she quieted.

I certainly didn't want to put that fear and hurt on Mama's face again while searching for our white people. She was my best friend, the confidante I talked with for hours, the one who still guided me when I lacked patience or common sense. I wouldn't turn the life she'd run from and then remade into a new horror for her. I decided, as painful as it would be for me, if we couldn't come to terms in the morning, there'd just have to be another way, at another time, to find out who my white family was.

———

The next morning, my parents and David were waiting for me downstairs on the plastic-covered green sofa, sipping coffee. Thank God Daddy was mellow, a sober look in his eyes and no Four Roses in sight yet. I got my coffee and sat in the orange chair across from them with my notebook and pen. Charles Nathan had opted out. No surprise.

I asked Mama if she was all right, after all we'd talked about the night before.

"I didn't sleep much," she said, as the dark circles under her eyes verified. "It's been so long since I left that all behind me, and I never expected this family to have to deal with it." Her thumbs twiddled at the speed of an electric mixer. "Even so, all kinds of memories have been spilling out of me the blessed night long. So, let's go ahead and talk about it a little. What do you want to know about my family?"

"Thank you, Mama. Thank you for talking to me about this. How about starting with who your people are and how you grew up?"

Her father was Henry Lewis, her stepmother was Mildred, and she had one sibling, a half sister, Dorothy, who was nine years younger. Her birth mother, who she had fond though faint memories of, died when Mama was four. I copied down their address, 635 Woodlawn Avenue in Indianapolis, Indiana, and their church, St. Patrick's Catholic parish, a few blocks away.

Her dad had seen to it there was enough for Catholic school fees even when money was short. He wanted her to have the best, and she went all the way through ninth grade at a Catholic girl's academy. "That was a darned good education for a girl in the '20s," she said. "Lots of girls I knew didn't go to high school at all."

I asked if all the classes were taught by nuns, or did they have lay teachers in parochial school back then?

"What do you need to know that kind of thing for? Are you going to want to dig into every single thing?"

It was just my way to know more about who she was as a girl, what white Catholic girls were like back then. A piece of what I came from. Anyway, what girl didn't want to know what her mother's youth was like?

She excused herself for a moment and went up to their bedroom. When Mama came back, she handed me a thin black-and-white booklet on glossy paper. Her ninth-grade yearbook! I couldn't believe she'd kept it in our house for fifty years yet we had never known it was there.

"You been holding out on us, Mama," David said.

Her class photo of lily-white, modestly dressed girls included the teacher-nuns in floor-length black habits, no hair showing. Mama was lovely and fresh, looking earnestly into the camera. Studying her face, I was struck that her gaze was like mine in my own high school yearbook. We had the same clear-eyed determination.

"Daddy was about as far from this world as you could get, wasn't he?" I said.

She and Daddy looked at each other, and he nodded. That's when they told us their outrageous story.

My father, Charles R. Jackson.

My mother, Ella Lewis Jackson.

Ella was working as the mail clerk at Holcomb's Electrical in 1942 when my father, the company handyman, was sent down there to build some badly needed storage shelves.

His mannerly greeting and the intelligent look in his eyes struck her first. He was nothing like the shiftless, ignorant people she'd heard colored people were. He seemed so decent, she decided to treat him like everybody else, Negro or not. She introduced herself and smiled at him as he carried in his supplies and tools.

Her smile confused Charles. He knew how to talk with exaggerated respect to white women in the South, but Ella's easy friendliness threw him. It seemed genuinely intended for him, like he was a real person to her, like she saw him as an actual man, not just some brown body to do work for her, the way whites always had treated him.

But what he didn't know were the unwritten rules between Negroes and whites in the North. And he sure didn't want any trouble. Relations between the races was supposed to be better in the North, but he hadn't figured out what that meant in Indiana. But like every black man, Charles knew any fraternization with a white woman had danger written all over it.

Ella saw he was neat and well groomed in his spotless, ironed work uniform. And as he used his level, saw, and hammer to make the shelves, he was efficient and good at what he did. She chatted with him about the increase in mail since the electrical business continued to grow and watched as Charles hoisted boxes up into place from a pile on the floor.

"I caught myself staring at his slim waist and broad shoulders," Mama said, "and how easily he lifted the heaviest boxes. He was nice and tall, five foot ten, and handsome. Your father was so strong and manly, I had to stop myself from looking at him."

Was this my proper mother talking, her mouth full of spice?

Over on the Negro side of town, Charles sat in his rented boardinghouse room most nights, stewing because he couldn't find a lady of his own. He was so lonely since coming to Indy. He left his first wife, the one in Buffalo he had to marry at seventeen when she said her baby was his, but afterward that it wasn't. In Indy, he didn't know many people and hadn't made any real friends. The silence of his room was suffocating him.

But it had been years now, and Charles was determined to have his own children with a good wife. He was thirty-six years old, trying to start life over. He didn't want to wait anymore. He just wanted to find a nice colored girl as soon as possible. But where could he find such a girl? He went to several Negro churches but mostly saw old ladies and younger women with kids. Being an unknown in town didn't help him make time with the few eligible girls he did see. Their mothers wanted to know where his people were, then snatched their daughters away when he said he was divorced.

"Those church girls weren't that pretty anyway," Daddy smirked. "The good ones were already taken."

The one he was looking for wasn't on Indiana Avenue at the Sunset Terrace either, where the brown sugar went to dance. They were good looking all right, sporting outfits that clung to their charms with jaunty hats tipped over done-up hair. The ones he talked to sho' 'nuff looked like sugar but their salty invitations tasted too much like his past.

So, Charles headed out to Madame C. J. Walker's Ballroom, *the* place for Indianapolis Negros to mingle. He was amazed that Walker's four-story building stretched down a whole block with several black businesses in it. On his way to the ballroom, Charles peeked into the empty theater that hosted jazz greats, plays, and other entertainments. It was themed with African décor, massive statues on either side of the stage, and plush red seat cushions! He marveled that a Negro could own anything that grand, let alone a Negro woman.

On to his mission, Charles continued toward the second-floor ballroom, adjusting his tie as the music got louder. Up there he found a tuxedoed band perched on a roulette wheel bandstand, shimmying out the fox-trot that couples danced to.

He took in the scene from the bar, his eyes flitting from one attractive girl in a fancy dress to another. As he sipped a too expensive shot of bourbon, another fellow eyed his broad shoulders and shined but worn shoes before coming over.

"See something you like?"

"Yeah, plenty," Charles said.

"Looky here, Jack," the man said. "Meeting a girl at Walker's depends on how much you got in your pocket and who your daddy is, see? And, if she ain't happy with both, all you're going to get is one dance, if you're lucky."

Charles watched smooth-talking men in stylish suits lead those women onto the dance floor, realizing he was out of his league. But since there was no law against watching the well-to-do's spectacle, he stayed a while for the jazz before taking a lonely stroll back to his boardinghouse.

All the way back, that white girl in the mail room at work ran through his mind. Like always. The one with guts enough to talk to him like a straight-up man. The one whose soft skin he imagined touching, even though the Klan would string up his damned fool self for looking at her, the way they did those two boys a few years ago out in the county. But man, oh man, wasn't she the sweetest woman he'd ever met?

The day came when Charles snuck down to the mail room and said the words to her he'd practiced in his mirror. "You don't mind talking to me, Ella? I mean, you seem comfortable with me. Are you a little afraid, maybe?" He wore a neutral smile, meaningless, in case she took offense.

"Oh, fiddlesticks, Charles, afraid of what? You're a nice man."

He stepped closer to her. "I hope I'm not out of line, but I want you to know that I like you. Very much."

She stared at him. Weighed his words intently. "I've thought of you too," she said.

At the sound of footsteps outside the door, Ella stepped back and began sorting letters at her mail table. Charles headed out the door just as the white man came in looking for a package.

But when Charles worked up his nerve again, he went back to the mail room during the slow part of the same day. "Ella, I want to ask you something," he whispered.

"Sure, you can ask me."

"Well, I've been wondering if you would want to see me, you know, outside of work?"

"You want to take me out?"

"Yes, I'd like to take you out somewhere nice, but you know we can't do that in public, don't you? A white woman and black man being seen together wouldn't be safe or smart. And I sure can't call on you at your house, where your family or friends would see me. So, the only thing I could come up with was to invite you to come over to my place. Would you want to spend some time with me? No fooling around, of course."

When she agreed to see him at seven on Saturday night, he handed her a slip of paper with his address. She should go to the train station first and then take a Negro cab from there to his place. That way no white cabbie who picked her up from her home would know where she went. He'd take care of the fare when she arrived.

He held his finger up to his lips. "Don't tell anybody."

"To tell the truth," Daddy told me, pouring a little Four Roses in his coffee, "by then I couldn't get your mother's dainty, ladylike ways out of my mind. And those beautiful dark curls I wanted to touch so bad . . ."

"OK, OK," I said. "But how did you end up getting married?"

"Well, see, I was divorced," Mama said. "And that had a lot to do with it."

"Wait," David said. "Say what now? You were married before too, Mama? To who?"

She'd married a Catholic from a neighboring parish that her parents thought was her last best chance. She was twenty-six and single, a certified old maid, after a previously broken engagement. She'd convinced herself Alan wasn't that pudgy or that short. Couldn't they learn to be happy, even if she and her groom were only friends?

But he and his family tricked her. He was past marrying age too, with no other prospects. During the courtship he entertained her with concerts and dinners, but his father was secretly paying for it all while he lied and said he had a job. He kept up that loafing when they were married, hardly working. And how he chased after other girls! He'd even brought one home for dinner, who was shocked to find out he had a wife. After she huffed out the door, Alan sat for days repeatedly playing "Come Back to Me" on their Victrola while he cried. Six years into their marriage, when Ella's younger sister Dorothy told her Alan had approached her too, Ella divorced him.

Mama told us a woman getting a divorce just wasn't done back then. Hers turned out to be a near disgrace. And no respectable Catholic man, the only kind her family would accept, would have her then. After all, a divorced and remarried woman could take a man down, all the way out of polite company. The Catholic Church, with a hard and fast doctrine opposing divorce, dictated that she would be excommunicated if she ever remarried.

Mama was bound to be a childless spinster, according to the church. But she had divorced because her husband was not what she always ached for: a responsible husband to have a family with. She was thirty-three years old and time was running out. She didn't know if she'd even be able to have children if she waited much longer.

That Saturday afternoon, Ella sat in the chintz chair in her own rented room, wondering about Charles. Should she take the chance, maybe a bigger risk than her decision to divorce had been, to get what she wanted—with a Negro? She knew there would be consequences, especially when she imagined Mother's face if she knew. But, yes, she was interested enough to get dressed up, put on some lipstick, and tell her landlady a lie about where she was going. This date would be her chance to find out whether a Negro, this specific Negro, was really a stand-up man.

When Ella's cab pulled up at his place, Charles was waiting on the sidewalk. As he helped her out of the taxi, the Negro cabbie turned all the way around in his seat to glare at Charles, who was opening her door.

"Man, why you want to mix me up in somethin' like this?" he asked.

"Just take the dollar," Charles said. "You haven't seen a thing, understand?"

He checked the boardinghouse hallway first to make sure nobody would see her. Then he showed Ella into his room of nicked furniture, a radio on a table with two chairs, and a hot plate on the kitchen counter. Behind a screen was a bed Ella could see was neatly made with hospital corners. The place was as clean as her impression of the man.

"Have any trouble getting here?" he asked.

The Negro cabbie asked her twice if she was sure of the address; if she wanted the colored side of town. Aside from that and his shaky smile, the ride had been fine.

She sat in the easy chair across from Charles.

"You know I've been to your house?" Charles asked. "Woodlawn Avenue, right?"

"What?" Ella stopped smiling and cleared her throat. "My dad knows you?"

No, they didn't know each other, really. The year before, her dad, who sometimes worked for Holcomb's, hired Charles to do yard work. It had been just that once, and he hadn't seen Ella there. "He was nice to me," Charles said. "I realized who he was today, when I connected your last names. Nice house, too."

"He's a wonderful father," Ella said. She told him her dad was a self-taught electrician, one of the early ones around town to make a living at it. He'd been part of the crew that initially wired up the Indianapolis Motor Speedway racetrack, and that got him work referrals by word of mouth.

"He doesn't know you're here, does he?" Charles asked nervously.

Of course, he didn't. And Ella promised to keep it that way.

She was more relaxed knowing her dad trusted Charles enough to hire him. So Ella told him about her stepmother, Mildred. She had consumption and never left the house, except to go to mass down the street. It was so bad that Ella's sister, Dorothy, had quit college to take care of Mildred, and Dad had to run a tab for her medicine at the drugstore. He knew not to expect his own family back in Ohio to help, even though they owned the Marshall drugstore chain. They had money, but they had disowned him when he married his first wife, Ella's birth mother. She stood too far down the ladder to suit people like them.

Charles handed Ella the Coke she had asked for before pouring a straight whiskey for himself. She raised her glass and made a toast.

> *Here's to it and to it again.*
> *If you don't do it when you get to it*
> *You may never get to it to do it again.*

"Where'd you learn something like that?" Charles said.

"That proves you don't know everything about me," she said, and laughed. "The fellas at the Catholic Thespian Society taught me that after our rehearsals. Anyway, no fools, no fun."

He liked the life in her eyes, the spirit in her soul. Without it, he realized, she never would have taken the chance to come see him.

Charles turned the radio to a moody blues tune, guitar wailing and harmonica crying. He patted his foot, digging the gravelly voice just before a colored announcer came on the air.

"Hey all you cats out there. It's Satidy night, time to get your best girl and cut a rug. Keep the dial right here, where the party keeps agoin' all night long."

Ella asked, "What channel's that? I've haven't heard radio like that before."

"I bet not," Charles said. "We Negroes have our own lingo, you know, jive talk."

She said, "No, I guess I don't know."

He pulled her up to dance to the radio, though she protested that she wasn't much of a dancer. Ella Fitzgerald's "A-Tisket, A-Tasket" was on, and much as they tried, neither could follow what the other was doing. Ella knew the fox-trot, with its set patterns, and Charles knew the country mule. They laughed through false turns and stepping on each other's feet. But when a slow tune came on, they did better. He folded Ella into his chest, and she followed his simple steps.

In no time, Charles and Ella were cooking dinner together at his place every Saturday night. After a few weeks, they added one more night a week, sometimes two. As they grew into love, Charles began to worry. He wasn't sure if she understood the trouble she could get in for being with him. Did a white girl know that somebody could attack her in the street if she was with him? Did she have any idea what she could face for breaking Jim Crow race laws and customs?

A number of Indianapolis and Marion County elected officials were open members of the Ku Klux Klan. They posed as the good guys, keeping the whites rightfully in power, and even did public service like giving away free food to needy whites. But did Ella understand that the Grand Wizard, a man name of Stephenson, used to run the nationwide hate mongering organization from Indianapolis? Did she know the Klan hated Negroes so much they terrorized and killed them?

She didn't.

Two Negro men, named Shipp and Smith, got lynched there in Marion County a few years before Charles and Ella took up. After a robbery and a murder, a white woman named Mary Ball claimed rape. The suspected men were locked up briefly, until a white mob broke into the jail with sledgehammers and strung them up.

Charles knew all about it, because he had seen a picture postcard of the lynching. It was taped up next to the price list at the black barbershop to warn customers. On it, a big crowd of whites, including women and children, milled around the brown bodies hanging from trees, their faces calm, satisfied. The victim's heads were bent over their nooses where their necks must have broken, and their limp legs swung free. They were left on display for the furious and curious to take in, as whites congratulated each other on delivering vigilante justice. It was proof, a man in the next barber's chair had told Charles, of how the Klan was the law in Indianapolis. "Don't take no chances in these parts," the man said. "The whites think the Klan is law abiding."

A studio photographer named Lawrence Beitler took the picture. As was the practice throughout the South, he sold thousands of copies, like circus souvenirs, to the white people. Charles also knew the aggrieved

Marion County, Indiana, lynching. *Indiana Historical Society*

Mary Ball later testified that she had not been raped, and that charge was dropped against the one surviving defendant who had managed to escape the lynching somehow. But the other two men were already dead, and nobody was ever charged with their murders.

Charles told Ella somebody could get the law on him for being with her, trump up charges and throw him in jail. Beat him half to death or string him up like those boys. And nobody would do anything about it, any more than they did for those who were lynched. He was getting pretty damned scared, and she should be too.

She had to understand that, at the very least, Holcomb's would surely fire him if it was ever found out they'd been together. Probably let her go as well. And if she thought her divorce had wrecked her name, being with him would mean worse. Not just the Catholics would turn their backs on her, all white people would.

"Mama, you really didn't know any of that?" David asked. "How in the world didn't you know?"

"My white corner of the world was completely sheltered from that kind of thing. Negro business wasn't my business, or anyone's I knew. My family didn't follow politics, or race, and even if they had, a lynching wasn't anything to talk to a young lady about. When your father explained all this to me, I had only the slightest idea."

David mopped his brow with a rough swipe. "Dang!" he said. "So, you didn't know black people were invisible in the '40s? Or that white people in your northern state went along with the Klan keeping them that way, same as down south. Unbelievable."

Charles wanted Ella to think those risks through before they saw each other again. She needed to decide if the risk of being together was worth it to her. She had to be sure she could live with never taking him home to her family for Christmas. Could she, and did she want to stay on her toes, alert and discreet so they never made that one mistake in public that would ruin her life? He had never been so serious.

Charles took Ella by the shoulders and finally said it, that he loved her. Loved her so much he was willing to face the danger to be with her. His forehead sweat and his voice dropped deep with desperation when he said he had to be sure she loved him like that too. He pulled her tight into his chest and stroked her thick curls as he bent to kiss her neck.

"Think hard before you answer me," he said. "I mean it."

6

A TRAIN RIDE

Ella was a praying woman who talked to God all day, every day. So, she took the joy and the misery of her love directly to God and the saints. The church that disowned her wouldn't be any help, but she still covered her head and went to a Catholic parish where nobody knew her to pray. In its dim light, Ella crept to the altar with a statue of Jesus looking down beatifically, his arms outstretched to comfort her. She lit a candle and sunk to her knees in supplication. She laid her life in the hands of the One who would never leave her. While an organist practiced in the loft, she prayed through several rosaries and begged, "Breathe on me, dear God, and tell me what to do."

Did He want her to stay single as the church demanded, or take another chance at love and her own family? Being with Charles would be dangerous if they weren't smart. But she loved him so. The alternative was a life as a damaged-goods spinster sentenced to take care of her stepmother. The one who'd treated Ella more like a ward than a daughter after Dad brought her home in his horse-drawn buggy with the fringed top.

She had already nursed her stepmother for years. Rise before six to bring a large pot of boiling water into Mother's darkened room for her to inhale the steam. Hold a tea towel covering both Mother's head and the pot until the steam softened the congestion in her chest. Gather and launder the hankies filled with yellow mucus and clots in runny lines. Fix all the meals. And evenings, help Mother sit up in her chair, feet on the heat register, to listen to the *Betty and Bob* radio soap opera before putting her back to bed.

She'd be poor no matter which life she chose. Charles didn't have anything, but they could both work and try to make something of their future. But her family had few prospects. Dad's sixteen-dollar-a-week salary and side jobs were barely enough to get by.

"I'm ready," Ella told Charles next time at his apartment. "I love you, and I'm ready to face whatever comes our way together. I trust you to take care of me and keep us safe."

"Will you marry me and make it legal?" Charles asked. "I want to come home to you every day."

She would. She would be very happy to be his wife.

He bent down to put his soft lips on hers, held her back, and kissed her deeply. She fell into him, tasting their future, surrendering to the love she had always wanted. She didn't care there would be no engagement ring. She couldn't wear it in public anyway. His promise to provide a home and love her were all she needed.

Mama told David and me that when she accepted him, she felt God smiling down on her. He wanted her to be happy. He would save her soul, just like he did Protestants who remarried.

———————

The following week on a lunch break at Holcomb's, Ella got a good look at the kind of risks Charles warned her about. That blonde Mary Jane from upstairs, with her tight sweaters, started the trouble with Jerome, the black man who worked on the loading dock.

Employees took their lunch out in back at the picnic tables under a sky of wispy clouds. Jerome's radio played Paul Whiteman, and he tapped his foot like a piston in rhythm, lost in his own pleasure. Everybody knew he loved to dance because Jerome's talk was all about the latest steps he'd mastered and the prizes he won in colored dance contests.

Mary Jane's foot tapped in double time as she snapped her fingers. Suddenly she jumped up and started a saucy sway on her way across to where Jerome sat. She grabbed his wrist firmly with two hands, pulling him up to his feet.

"Come on here, Jerome," she said. "Dance with me. I can keep up with your fancy footwork any day."

He tried to pull away gently, deferentially calling her Miss Mary Jane. Jerome smiled and said he didn't want to dance right then, but thanks just the same. He didn't think work was the right place for dancing. But she insisted, throwing her strength into pulling him. She made some jitterbug moves and Jerome gave way into stiff, reluctant turns, this way and that. When she kicked up her leg, some of her milky white thigh showed. The man was doing everything he could not to touch her. Oblivious, Mary Jane's shoulders thrust forward with a shimmy and then dipped backward, as he stood paralyzed.

He backed away slowly. "You won, Miss Mary Jane, you sure did win. You're the best." He smiled nervously, aware of his coworkers' stormy expressions. The lunch whistle blew, and Mary Jane sauntered off, swishing her hair back off her face as her lips pulled wide, relishing her moment.

As soon as she was gone, the white men moved toward Jerome. Sweating, he put his hands out in a gesture of "I don't want no trouble." But the foreman shouldered his way in front of Jerome and faced the crowd, ordering the men to knock it off. "We got work to do," he shouted. "Better go on and git to it." As the grumbling crowd dispersed, the red-faced foreman with a large bald spot grabbed Jerome by his collar and pulled him into his office.

Charles hid inside a doorway, watching from where he couldn't be seen, then disappeared inside. For days, the white men complained that the foreman should've let them teach that porch monkey to never touch a white woman. They didn't know why the boss even let niggers work near white women. But those men never got their chance, because Jerome was never seen on the premises again.

Charles made himself scarce around Holcomb's, kept his head down, and said nothing. He stopped going anywhere near the mail room.

———————

Now that Ella had said yes, Charles turned over idea after idea to find a way to marry and live without fear. It wasn't until he confided to his mother in Buffalo that a plan took shape. His mom's shock had turned to support once he made her understand that he would marry Ella, no matter what. In the end, it was his mom's idea he ran with.

Charles told Ella their best chance was to run away. They would start over in a new place where nobody would bother them. A place the law wouldn't get them.

"What do you say, Babe?" he asked, clutching her hand as if to keep her from running. "Will you go with me?"

"You mean leave Indianapolis, don't you?"

He knew she wouldn't want to leave her family. Nor the only place she'd ever lived. Charles had to break it down for her and went step by step. Did she know that a black-white marriage was illegal in Indiana? Or that they could both go to jail for intermarrying—miscegenation they called it. The sentence was years in prison, as much as seven years of hard labor for both the woman and the man.

She pulled away from him. Was it as bad as all that?

Indiana was the lone northern state in America to keep antimiscegenation laws on the books past 1888. Mixed marriage remained illegal there nearly seventy years longer than in any neighboring states, until its repeal in 1965. Learning this as a result of researching my parents' story proved the supposedly free North practiced the same Jim Crow as the South.

Charles meant not only leaving Indy, but also not telling her family. Not now, not ever. If her dad knew where they went, he could have Charles arrested, and everything he feared might happen anyway, including prison or death. He said her family wouldn't accept him, not even from a long distance. Not only could the family put a stop to their marriage, but she needed to understand how much her family's lives would be affected by her marrying him.

He said white people would shun her family for what she did. Her dad wouldn't get those extra jobs and might even lose the work he already had. Then how would he provide for his sick wife and family? If her mother knew Ella was with Charles, it could kill her in her weakened state. If Mother didn't call the law on them first. As much as Ella didn't want to leave Dorothy, did Ella realize how badly Ella being with Charles would hurt Dorothy's reputation and marriage prospects? No upstanding Catholic man would marry into such a tainted family.

Charles insisted she could never let them know. The way to keep them in the dark was to move to a new state where nobody knew them. They would go to New York, at his mother's suggestion. Interracial marriage was legal there, and they could live together in the open. He had a brother in New York they could build a new life with. His family would be her family.

"Mama, how could you bear to leave your people?" I asked, touching her arm. "You must have been so miserable."

"I decided to marry your father. And I wouldn't ruin my family's lives for that choice. I still believe it was the only choice we had." Her voice broke. She pulled the Kleenex out from her sleeve, ready for any tears. "They could get over me leaving . . . in time . . . we'd all have to."

"And you've never contacted them since? Not ever?"

"We never looked back," Daddy said, yanking his head down in a nod of finality.

"Refugee lovers," David said, slapping his knee. "Undercover all these years." He could dig it.

I sat in the living room looking at these plain, hardworking people who led such a simple existence. I'd never really seen them. Never given them credit for having that kind of grit and courage. Never understood their belief in love over race was trailblazing.

Mama and I spent the afternoon doing Saturday chores together, shopping and washing before she started dinner. Daddy peeled potatoes and I snapped green beans as we picked up their story. Daddy had gotten into it, ready now to tell it all.

"What the hell," he told Mama. "Why not tell? Dolores is going to do right by us with whatever she decides to do." He stopped peeling. "We have your word on that, right?"

I assured him they did.

———————

In spring 1943, Ella insisted to her skeptical family that traveling alone to go visit her high school friend in Massachusetts would be safe. She wanted to get away for a while. Away from all the Indy folks who'd dropped her after the divorce.

Her dad said from the first mention of the trip that he disapproved of a young lady traveling halfway across the country unaccompanied. She didn't know anything about New England or their ways. Ella was a Midwesterner after all.

"Even so," Mama said, "my dad knew he couldn't convince me when my mind was made up. He hadn't been able to talk me out of getting divorced, so he gave in and took me to the train station."

Henry Lewis looked lost as he and Dorothy stood on the station platform, putting Ella on the train headed east. Mother, of course, was too sick to come. Ella took that moment to memorize her loved one's faces. All she could take of them were the images of Dad's too-prominent nose, and Dorothy's innocent face. The roughness of her dad's hand and the softness of her sister's when she squeezed them, the care and concern in their hugs and kisses. She'd need those memories, to take them out and study their details all the rest of her years.

Ella should come home early if she got homesick, Dad said. Otherwise they'd look for her in Indy by Memorial Day. She gave him a bright smile and cheery wave.

Once the train pulled out and her family disappeared, Ella watched the budding trees and farms roll by. Her initial melancholy was quickly overtaken by the rush she felt knowing that nobody had caught on to her plan. Good-bye to Indiana forever, she thought. Good-bye to my philandering ex-husband and the self-righteous Catholics who shunned me for divorcing him. Good-bye to the narrow-minded people who would punish her family for her being with a Negro, the Klan who would hurt Charles, and the laws that made their marriage illegal. She'd erase their power and marry who she wanted.

The ride comforted her, as the loud rumble and jostle of the rocking train running away with her seemed to give voice to her thrill, shouting, "Freedom! Freedom!"

Already at work in Buffalo, Charles was nervous as a jackrabbit. He was waiting to see if Ella would fool her family or, God forbid, get cold feet. She was due in New York City that day, where he'd gone first and stayed in Harlem with his older brother Marion. But the strain of the dock job he got there ripped the hernia that had already disqualified him from the army. He'd moved on to Buffalo where his mom could look after him a while. Then, when healed, he decided to stay in Buffalo where he got a decent welder's job.

Ella rode the train through Indiana, Ohio, and New York, arriving in Manhattan as planned. At a telephone booth in Grand Central Station, she dialed Charles's mother in Buffalo to find out her next move.

Belia answered, speaking to Ella in the sweet voice she saved for tender moments. Charles would be so happy she made it to New York, she said. But now there was a change of plans. Ella was to take another train and come on up to Buffalo, the next day if possible.

"You got enough money to get here?" Belia asked.

"Yes, I do. Thanks."

"Then I'll be glad to meet you when you do, honey."

Ella stopped for the night at a hotel in Times Square. She walked around the area for a while and found her evening meal close by. The painted prostitutes in doorways and crowds of lewd men and rubbernecking tourists roaming up and down Forty-Second Street fascinated

Ella at first. But the urine-soaked doorways and greasy-haired men who paid her too much attention drove her back into the hotel. She was glad she and Charles wouldn't be living in New York after seeing its underbelly.

Ella filled out the hotel postcard she found in her room's desk drawer, telling her family she was having a good trip and had stopped for the night. She wrote that she missed them already and loved them. It was to be her last word to them. That way, there could be no questions, no interference, no more lies. She and Charles had agreed that was best. The family would get over her disappearance faster if they couldn't find her.

She called Charles when he was home from work. Yes, he was well now. He'd meet her train, and they'd stay with his mom until Ella found a job and moved into a rented room. That would only be until arrangements for their wedding could be made.

By morning, Ella had disappeared from her family. She was on the train to Buffalo where nobody would ever find her, to marry a man nobody knew she was involved with.

The afternoon of June 19, 1943, Ella tidied up the display of kitchen linens in her section of Nora's Dime Store. With the last customer gone and the cash drawers accounted for, she wished everyone a good weekend and dashed out the door. She hadn't breathed a word to her coworkers about Charles, let alone her wedding that night. She'd already learned to keep that to herself, because even people in Buffalo, where interracial marriage was legal, were against it. Seemed like just about everybody was.

At her rooming house on Elmwood Avenue she got into her aqua dress with the white lace collar. She added the petite white hat and veil, dashed some lily of the valley toilet water behind her ears. After checking that every detail looked perfect in the mirror, she finally slipped into white heels and gloves. When she came downstairs to meet Charles in the parlor, he let out a low whistle and laid his hat over his heart. While

Ella bid good-bye to the landlady, who wished them well, Charles took her suitcases to the waiting cab.

Reverend Sydney Johnson, who would preside over the ceremony in his living room, reviewed the marriage license before starting. Belia and her man, Jimmy Thomas, were the witnesses and only guests. When Belia had approached the minister about officiating, he was apprehensive. She wanted him to marry a colored and a white together? The way white folks carried on about race mixing, and most Negroes too, he didn't really want to do it. But the couple had pledged to become members of his flock like Belia was, so what could he say? The reverend prayed there would be no trouble in the congregation about this that would empty his pews or the collection plates that he'd spent so many years building up. During the ceremony, though, he had to admit that Ella was a woman in love, and Charles was bursting with pride as they made their pledges. He hoped it would be enough to see them through what they would most certainly have to endure.

They took a cab back to Belia's rear rental flat on Hickory Street to celebrate with fried fish and love songs on the kitchen radio. When Ella said how good the fish tasted, Belia told her to come on by so she could learn her how to cook Charles's favorites.

My grandmother Belia.

"You can start calling me Mom, like he does," Belia said. "I'll be your mama now." Before they left for the room Charles rented, Belia kissed them. She said they both needed somebody to love, and she was happy they found each other. "I'm gonna do what I can to help you," she said. "But you got to be strong. This ain't gonna be easy."

On their walk home, Charles asked, "You know what my mother said about you before the wedding? She said 'That's one brave white girl you got there. She sho' 'nuff loves you. And that's all I needs to know 'bout her.'"

I have wondered so many times, what made my parents step out so far on hopes and dreams. Would they have seriously considered marrying if they had foreseen what lay ahead of them?

A few weeks after the wedding, Cousin Rosalie was having a birthday bash. Charles said Rosalie was such a live wire the party was going to be out of sight, with dancing till dawn and the best down-home cooking you ever tasted. All the uncles, aunts, cousins, and who-so-evers were coming.

"I wanted to go to a party so bad," Mama said to David and me, stretching her short legs out under the coffee table. She and Daddy had spent all their time with just Grandma and Jimmy for weeks. "I wanted to meet the family and have some laughs."

"Yeah," Daddy said, rolling his eyes. "We wanted some laughs."

Belia told Ella she wouldn't enjoy the crowd much. It wouldn't be her kind of music. Instead, why didn't they come to her place for dinner that night? But Charles wasn't about to miss that much fun.

The night of the party, Charles started on his Four Roses as he snapped his polishing cloth over the toes of his shoes. He wanted to look good when he and Ella walked in. He'd looked over her dresses and suggested the one he liked best on her, and at the last minute, pulled off his stocking cap to admire the smoothed down waves it made in his hair.

They walked over with Belia and Jimmy and found Rosalie in her front yard.

"Hey, baaaby!" the near six-foot, coal-black woman in a red flounced dress called. "Looky here, it's my cousin or nephew or whosonever kin you is, Charles. And this here must be your new wife. How you doing, girl? Come on in; we're gonna party down!" Her hips gyrated like a lawnmower to the bebop music spilling out of the house.

The crowd was all Negro, as Ella expected. But what she wasn't ready for was the way people stared at her without any acknowledgement or smile. One man's mouth hung open, his eyes following her through the room. She overheard him say, "What's that white woman doing here?"

She, Charles, and Belia made their way through a crowd of dancers trying to outdo each other. Some of them moved with a hypnotic abandon to the record pulsating with horns and drums. It looked so exciting, Ella playfully wiggled her eyebrows up and down at Charles on the way to the kitchen to meet Belia's brother, Butch.

Butch's voice boomed above the noise, bragging about how good his BBQ sauce had come out. "I put my foot in it," he said, praising himself in the highest, a toothpick bobbing from the corner of his mouth. The man was built solid, had a pockmarked face, and wore a stingy brim black hat with a small feather in the band. His signature, that hat never came off, except in church.

Belia whispered to Ella that Butch thought he ran things in the family. "But I runs the family around here, and Butch just runs his mouth." She introduced Ella, and Butch nodded, making a barely audible grunt.

Butch's wife, Edna, an amiable seamstress, gave Ella a smile and invited her to come over for coffee sometime. But before Ella could reply, Butch jerked around and said Edna better check with him about any invitations.

Belia stepped up in Butch's face. "Don't start," she said. "We done talked about this."

He stared back, but before he could say anything, a pretty woman in a formfitting dress appeared, leaning against the kitchen doorway. With a sweep of her extended arm at the kitchen gathering, she curled the left side of her lip and raised an eyebrow, sneering.

"I didn't believe Charles would have the balls to bring his white woman out in front of us tonight. Ain't that some nerve?" she asked nobody in particular. Charles stepped between his first and second wives and suggested his ex should go up front to have her fun, where people would be happier to see her.

"Just 'cause dark meat ain't good enough for you no more, don't mean you can bring your white trash here where folk are trying to have a party. Who wants to look at her?"

"It was terrible," Mama said. "I hadn't seen that kind of prejudice against whites before. I was in the middle of all these Negroes who knew her and not me. I thought we should leave, but Daddy didn't move."

"This rude woman is my ex-wife," Charles told Ella. "Now you can understand why I wouldn't want to be married to her."

Butch started yelling the one volume he seemed to have, cursing Charles. It wasn't bad enough that he'd married a white woman and run away with her. He was trying to get them all killed when the law or her daddy came with a gun looking for her.

His ex chimed in. Wasn't their marriage against the law? Looked like Charles had forgotten his own fool nigger place. But the rest of them hadn't forgotten theirs. They knew what a mad peckerwood could do to a nigger. And why did Charles think any of these party people wanted to meet Ella when no white folks had ever been a friend of theirs?

"Dammit, y'all quit it now," Belia said. She had her hands on her hips and a look in her eyes that put the fear of God in them. "Ain't I already told you not to jump all over them? Can't you so-called church niggers show some Jesus in you? We got a new member of the family here, married good and legal."

Butch knocked that bowl of thick barbeque sauce over, and red splatters dribbled down the wall. Then he jumped in front of Charles, toe-to-toe with his clenched fists raised. Charles nudged Ella into a corner and stood ready to take on his uncle. His ex watched from her perch against the door, looking mighty satisfied.

Rosalie came running in, asking if these niggers had lost their minds, fighting in the middle of her birthday. "Stop this right now," she said, pulling on Butch. "Don't y'all break none of my stuff. And don't anybody call the cops. You knew she was coming," she said, cutting her eyes to Ella, hanging back in her corner.

Belia pushed Charles aside and poked Butch in his barrel chest. Said he had to apologize. He glared, his lips glued together. Until he apologized, Belia didn't want to hear another word from him. "You need to take that five-dollar hat off your five-cent head till you get some sense in it," she said.

She turned to Charles and Ella. "You need to listen to me when I say no. Charles, you should've known who was going be here. And that Butch would act like an eggbeater in a cesspool. You better smarten up if you don't want this kind a trouble."

The partygoers argued among themselves and took sides. Some said Charles and Ella hadn't done anything to them; give the white girl a chance. Others said Charles deserved to get his ass kicked for bringing a white woman there. What did she want with them anyway?

The family and community stayed split on whether to let Ella into their lives for a long time. Some made it their business to avoid her until the close relatives let up some. Aunt Edna had Ella over for coffee anyway, when Butch wasn't home. She joined forces with Belia to get others to see Ella was all right.

In time, they were at the all-family Christmas breakfast every year, eating the brains-and-eggs scramble Uncle Butch made special for the holiday. And Rosalie's kids, who were similar ages to my brothers and I, were our birthday party guests. But some never got in the boat.

On Christmas six months later, Ella and Charles woke to bright sun spilling over a wintry cold day. They had scrambled eggs she made on the hot plate in their room and listened to carols on the radio as they exchanged gifts of perfume and cologne.

Then Ella opened the surprise gift the two gay men downstairs had given her. She was touched by the thin tea towels inside the Santa Claus wrapping paper. That show of kindness reciprocated her plate of Christmas cookies a few days before. They had a community in that tenement, where each person's humanity was recognized with kindness and respect, no matter what they faced out on Buffalo's intolerant streets.

Ella described how back in Indianapolis the family would have gone to midnight mass on Christmas Eve to see the baby Jesus in the crèche. Then back home, they'd have opened a little present and eaten Mother's date nut cookies before bed.

"Are you sad, babe?" Charles asked. "You must miss them something terrible today."

"Oh, horsefeathers, Charles. I miss them, sure, but you know very well I'm not sad." She rubbed her growing belly. "You just want me to tell you again that you and the baby are the most important things in my life."

Daddy smiled across the living room at David and me. "That was Charles Nathan she was carrying," he said. "We moved to Hickory Street a few houses down the block from Grandma to that rear flat where you were little. Then you came, David, and then you, Dolores. You know the rest."

Charles and Ella with firstborn, Charles Nathan.

David, Charles Nathan, and Dolores, Easter, 1952.

The next morning, I told my parents about the class on finding your family, where I'd learned how to search for our white folks.

"You went to school on this before you even came home to talk to us?" Daddy asked.

"Yeah, but I did come and ask you before going any further. As it turns out, I might have a business trip to Indianapolis in the next few months. I'm thinking about staying afterward to look for the Lewises."

"That soon?" Mama said. "We're just getting used to the idea and you're halfway out the barn door already. It's just like you not to have an ounce of patience. But you must remember you made me a promise."

"I'll keep you out of this. Don't worry."

We agreed I'd need more details to pull off the search. So, luckily, my parents filled in a lot more blanks in the following weeks. In fact, Mama called the very next day with Daddy on the extension.

"Hey," she said, "we thought of something else important you should know . . ."

7

BLACK GIRL

M y head had to be on straight before going to Indianapolis to
find my white people. If the missing Lewises could be found,
I wondered how hard it would be, not only to get through the shocking news I'd deliver, but also to relate to each other. How would they
deal with a black woman like me who wore a millstone of race trouble
around my neck, held on a heavy chain of resentment and suspicion?
There was no telling who and what we would see when we looked on
each other the first time.

After all, the confines of ghetto life racism I experienced growing
up taught me that blacks could not be part of the wider city life. When
my five-year-old self fell against our coal-burning pot-bellied stove and
my arm sizzled against the cast iron like bacon in a frying pan, the
white cab company lied about sending a cab right over. Instead they
left Mama and I waiting on the frozen Buffalo sidewalk as my skin rose
into delicate black meringue peaks.

We lived on Hickory Street, with people packed into substandard
rentals like crackers in a sleeve. The block had vacant lots full of debris,
a pushcart selling greasy hot tamales, and numbers-running men taking
bets all day then calling out winners in a supper time evensong.

Our living room ceiling cracked from the raucous upstairs neighbors' rent parties. Then one Christmas morning a sharp snap brought a
deluge of plaster down all over us, knocking the tree over while burying

the opened presents. Instead of a happy celebration, we swept, washed furniture, walls, and clothes, finally dumping chunks of the ceiling and the desert of dust into the garbage. Our white landlord didn't return Daddy's calls and never came to fix anything. First Daddy had a few drinks and raged about it, then he set up two wooden work horses in the living room, got on a ladder, and made us a new ceiling himself. When Daddy took the bus to answer a rental ad for a better apartment, the owner had shouted, "No niggers!" and shut the door. We knew white people didn't want us near them. We also knew Daddy was so enraged that something as small as spilling a glass of milk or pulling a chair out from under each other could turn his humiliations into our whippings with his welding shop's discarded leather strap.

That sealed off ghetto life told me blacks were not to expect the basics, let alone extra or different. We were supposed to accept the less-than life white people had us boxed into, the life racism would never let me out of. That made me want to get out of their box, but not get out of the black community where my little black self was nurtured by a sense of understanding one another. I didn't feel boxed in by my black playmates or my black grandma down the street or eating the grits and collard greens that had migrated north too.

Getting good grades in school felt like getting out of white people's box because it defied their belief that we were stupid and lazy. By eighth grade we had moved to a less segregated neighborhood, and I often spent afternoons studying at Jay Berman's house, the boy who vied with me for first place in everything.

Jay, the lone white kid in that grade, lived a few blocks away in a house full of the books and magazines his dad read. Daddy said he didn't work because McCarthy's House Un-American Activity Committee had blacklisted him even though they never proved he was a communist.

One day when our homework ran late, I jumped up to go see *Amos 'n' Andy* on TV, the sitcom about ignorant blacks. Mr. Berman said he was surprised at me. "You shouldn't watch a thing like that. It makes fun of your people, and of you," he said. "Negroes aren't ridiculous like the characters on that show. It makes white people think your hardworking father and you are like that just because you're Negro."

The show was so funny, I'd never seen it as denigrating my race, and neither had the many African Americans who half-believed those white prejudices themselves. Mr. Berman asked if I'd ever known a Negro as ludicrous as Lightnin', the shuffling ignoramus on the show.

"Nobody's that stupid," I said.

"A smart girl like you can do well in life if you know better than to accept nonsense like *Amos 'n' Andy*. Choose what you fill your head with very carefully."

"How should I choose?" I asked.

"Get a good education, Dolores. That will teach you how to think for yourself. Then you can figure out most anything. What's in your head determines who you are."

But at home, Daddy and David had an *Amos 'n' Andy* routine, falling out laughing as they reenacted the idiocy. David shuffled across the floor, scratching his hangdog head, speaking country bumpkin Ebonics with an IQ of sixty-five.

"What's 'a matter, dere, Lightnin'?" Daddy asked, playing the scheming Kingfish. "Don'tcha want ter trade your car for a bridge?"

I told them what Mr. Berman said, but David kept right on. "Be cool. It's just a joke."

But it wasn't funny anymore, so I stopped watching. Years later I understood that mockery was created by white people. It fed prejudice against African Americans during its popular run on radio and CBS TV for thirty years until it went off air in the 1950s. That institutional racism was sponsored by products like Campbell's Soup and Pepsodent toothpaste, broadcast into millions of homes where its disparagement was presented as entertainment.

By the time us kids in the 'hood were bussed from a Sears Roebuck parking lot on the Jefferson Special to the white Bennett High School across town, I was black to the bone. We called that old repurposed city bus the Ghetto Express because it drove straight to a neighborhood of well-to-do white people in large brick homes and back to the 'hood with no stops allowed.

During the ride, boys played the dozens, trying to outdo each other's outrageous insults about one another's mothers. We girls, the intended audience, cheered the most brash wisecracks and pooh-poohed those that fell flat, egging them on until one of them was out of comebacks.

"Yo' mama's so short she poses for trophies."

"Yeah, well yo' mama so fat she got her own zip code."

At Bennett, a school with about six hundred in each grade, we ghetto kids started the day mixed in with white kids. During the brief homeroom period, we sat in wooden one-piece desks and chairs for attendance and announcements. When the class bell rang, I was separated from my friends to spend the day as one of few, or sometimes the only, black kids in honors classes.

I held back in those classes at first, worried I didn't belong there, because these kids were white. White kids who had everything, knew everything, and whose entitlement said that was how it was supposed to be. White kids who chattered with each other and planned get-togethers as I sat silently by, invisible. White kids who had already read the books on the reading list.

But when I was the only one to answer a question about *Julius Caesar* in Old English, I changed my mind. Riding home later on the Ghetto Express, I sat with one of the dozens players the school had put in shop classes making shoeshine or bread boxes.

"What's happenin', Madame Butterfly?" he said. The kids nicknamed me that in elementary school, labeling me an egghead, a "proper" young lady, with an older brother who'd made it plain nobody was to mess with me.

"I'm reading Shakespeare."

He cracked up. "Naw you ain't. For real girl, what you up to?"

Those honors classes created a personal push and pull about my "place" all through high school. While I couldn't have explained it back then, many of my Ghetto Express friends were being taught to live with the lower-class circumstances of our birth, while honors classes were opening new worlds to me. At fourteen, our futures were being determined by the tracks we were put in.

On the Ghetto Express, I threw in with some hip girls planning to join the Bennett drill team and perform at football game halftime shows. An older black girl had convinced the white coach to add some soul to the routines, and it was our mission to make them sooo fly.

At rehearsals I was lined up in a row of the school auditorium with the short girls, some white, some black, to learn the steps. Our black leader was up front showing how to rock a long step forward and sway back on the other foot with funky attitude. Her rolling hips amazed.

The team began the move, but not together. We black girls got into the groove and strutted our stuff. Some of the white girls did it, but others were reluctant, trying to make the move fit the team's previous military marching style, as was school tradition. A head bop was added. The white girl next to me looked disapproving and didn't do it.

After a few practices, the old military marching team was nowhere to be seen and the white girls had all quit. We added our sassiest steps in the aisle of the Ghetto Express, ignoring the driver shouting at us to sit down. Before long, we'd won our version of a civil rights coup. That white school had an all-black drill team, jammin' with homegirls' steps.

I wondered if my white relatives, should I meet them, would be able to respect me for finding triumph in those halftime shows. I also wondered if the Lewises could relate to my mixed race. Lots of folks couldn't, as I learned back in high school.

One Saturday I skipped the drill team performance to sit bunched together with the black kids in All-High Stadium at a Bennett game. We were separated from the white students by mutual choice. Sprawled out behind me was an elementary classmate, a boy so black complexioned he was nearly blue. While everyone stood for the national anthem he sat, loudly running his game on a white girl so blonde I had to study her face to see if she had eyelashes.

I turned and touched my finger to my lips. "The national anthem is playing."

"Shut the fuck up, you sorry half-breed," he said.

Me?

With a forced a smirk I turned around, and caught the astonished look on the face of a red-headed white boy from honors class. The black kids tittered and watched to see if we'd fight, as our neighborhood code called for. Truth was, Madame Butterfly had never fought anybody. I pretended the incident was meaningless, cheering and chatting until I could escape at halftime.

But inside, I could hardly think straight. I shouldn't have called his behavior out, but why did he have to name me as less than our black crew? I'd thought the whole Ghetto Express crowd were my boon-coons. Like the grooves of a 45 RPM record my mind looped: DoIbelong? DoIbelong? DoIbelong?

Mama was seasoning chicken when I got home and told her what had happened. She cleared her throat then said, "Don't take that race bait, Dolores. Life's hard enough without worrying about what people say about your being mixed. Ignore it, like I do."

That boy's two-by-four upside my head cracked my identity open. Everybody didn't accept me as the black I thought I was. The specter of that uncertain acceptance would stay with me always, leaving me to wonder which blacks might harbor similar resentment.

In later years, I had another such incident, during an after-work drink with some black corporate colleagues. We took a table in the back where we could talk quietly, away from the noisy yuppies at the bar. There had been an incident where another black coworker shouted at the vice president that he was tired of working on a corporate plantation.

One man said I didn't know how bad it really was because the white management accepted me more than darker coworkers. "Your skin's so light, and you speak so proper you sound white."

"I'm as black as you, and you know it," I said, unaware in those days of my light-skinned privilege.

"My high yellow sistah, so you say." He wanted me to agree The Man could relate to my similarity with the wives and daughters he had at home. He beat a rhythm on the tabletop and chanted:

If you're light, you're all right.
If you're brown, stick around.
But if you're black, get back.

Others accused me of thinking I was better than them because I was light. Black men told me how fine I was because I was "light, bright, and damned near white." Darker men flattered my looks, saying I'd make a good choice as a wife. Having a fair-skinned wife would give them some status, and importantly, make their children lighter.

But I saw myself as black, no matter what they said. My father told us we were. "You kids have light skin and straight noses because your mother's blood is stronger than mine. But you're black, you're always going to be black, and the white man is never going to let you forget it."

David was probably right. Meeting with my lost white relatives could backfire because of race. But I was still ready to risk that, because even if we couldn't relate to each other, that too was part of knowing whose blood ran in my veins.

And yet, the day I helped a shy blonde transfer student find her locker I had no expectation of making a white friend. A white friend who would teach me that race didn't have to matter between individuals. Jackie Milligan was all soft-spoken refinement, a balm to the no-holds-barred acting out that was our normal on the Ghetto Express. She seemed honest and easy, and accepted me without judgement.

"What's happenin', Jackie," I'd say, the slang making her giggle. When we were together, people's eyes darted back and forth over us. She was five foot nine and thin; I was five foot two and overweight. She was delicate and reserved; I was rough and forward. Both of us wore glasses, were nerds in honors classes, and took piano lessons. Somehow, we made sense of things together—I brought her out of her shy ways, and she led me into her world of yachts and horses.

Her mom, a genteel spirit, drove us to their three-story brick house after school one day. It sat on a quiet street with a grassy median, so unlike my street with its multifamily units and a factory down the block. Jackie showed me her toy horse with a hair tail that resembled the real horse she had to leave behind in Michigan. All I knew about horses was my one pony ride, the animal led by a man around a circle at a fair.

When her dad came home, her mom served cookies with tea in a china pot wrapped in a tea cozy. Who knew there was such a thing? Like a British movie, we sat near the grand piano in their long living room, the teapot resting on a gold filigree coffee table.

Jackie sat down at the piano, tearing into the theme from *Lawrence of Arabia*. She threw her head back and her long hair hung behind her. A fantasy played on her face as the music became a story of desert races I could hear. That music moved her as much as Motown did me. In the 'hood, we made fun of classical and other forms of "white" music. But the way Jackie played it, I found the feeling and beauty for the first time.

I rubbed my finger across the gold filigree table. "This is so beautiful," I said.

"Oh this? We got that in Egypt on our trip around the world," Mr. Milligan said.

They went around the world? The farthest I'd gone was Harlem, to visit Daddy's relatives. The highlight was getting autographs at the stage door of the Apollo Theater on 125th Street.

The Milligans talked casually about the Taj Mahal, getting separated in the broiling sun at the Egyptian pyramids, and having high tea in London. They laughed about elephant rides and Africans staring at their white skin, the way Daddy talked about the pro wrestling matches downtown.

From then on, it was like the Milligans adopted me. And what an education they gave me, wrapped in love. As Jackie's companion, they took me to several cultural performances. We saw Van Cliburn play piano at Kleinhans Music Hall, from seats where we could watch his long fingers fly and his delicate wrists float up from the keyboard after the last note. We saw a performance of *Carmen* where the sets and elaborate military and Spanish costumes awed. But what surprised me most about the opera, which I thought was the ultimate in dignified art, was the hussy who was pure trouble.

"My dear," Mr. M. said, his eyes twinkling, "operas are full of hussies and scoundrels, just like real life."

The Milligans took me out on their yacht one weekend, where we girls swam in the river and lunched at the cabin dining table. I even drove the boat in the river's calm waters that would become violent rapids that rushed over Niagara Falls. At home at their dinner table, Mr. M. held court, discussing what was at stake in national elections, Martin Luther King Jr.'s versus Malcom X's philosophies, and the import of Cesar Chavez's United Farm Workers strike.

They showed me that the world held so many more options than I could ever have imagined from inside the sealed off ghetto mentality. What the Milligans gave me was not a desire for their custom ruby crystal wine glasses from Lido, Italy, but how they thought. They showed me how to do what Mr. Berman urged me to do—think for myself and fill my head with worthwhile ideas.

Mama said we should invite the Milligans to our house some evening when she was off, to show some hospitality and appreciation. Daddy worried we couldn't pass a whole evening with such educated, well-to-do people. What in the world could we talk about?

"Anything you want," Mama said. "Dolores talks with them, so we can too. They're just people."

Mama and I dressed up in stockings and patent leather heels and Daddy had on a white long-sleeved shirt and tie. Mama excused my brothers because Jackie was my friend, not theirs. She made an expensive crab dip to impress, and Daddy, who already had a few Four Roses beforehand, placed the bottle in the center of the coffee table. I crossed my fingers he wouldn't get drunk.

"Have one with me, Mr. Milligan?" he asked as soon as they were settled.

"Absolutely, pour me one please."

Mr. M., who loved politics, asked Daddy if he liked President Lyndon Johnson.

"I gotta be for him, for all he's done for the civil rights bills."

"Better than Goldwater, huh?" Mr. M. asked.

"That bastard? He's against the unions," Daddy said. "I'm the sergeant at arms for the local Steelworkers, you know."

Mr. M. raised his glass in a salute.

Daddy took me to a union meeting once when there was nobody at home to keep me. There, an all-white crowd of men got loaded in the bar before a boisterous meeting upstairs to take a strike vote. Daddy was so worried about them getting out of control, he sat me next to the exit so we could run out if fighting broke out. "A black sergeant at arms can't make angry white men behave," he said.

Mr. M. gently jiggled his empty glass for another Four Roses. Daddy was happy then. He had a man to drink and talk shop with. They toasted each other a few times, Mr. Milligan matching Daddy drink for drink. When the Milligans stood up to go, Daddy pumped Mr. M.'s hand a long time.

"Gee, Mr. Milligan," he said. "I had no idea educated people could be so much fun!"

My high school life was not all yachts and opera. By age sixteen, I worked after school as a second-shift aide at a nursing home. A yellow pinafore uniform that repelled liquids and stains was required, the reason for which I quickly learned. My job, along with the rest of the all black staff, was to get the elderly patients on the dementia ward, all of whom were white, washed and put to bed. I had entered the servant class.

The residents had limited mobility and little understanding of the realities of their lives. Those capable of holding a conversation I could follow thought we were way back in time, when they were younger. Like Blanche, who talked to me in a booming voice as if I were one of her elementary school students. As I pushed her wheelchair into the bathroom and set her on the toilet, she would instruct me. I worked steadily to wash her face and hands as she kept on: "Time to go over your homework." I answered math problems while removing her dress, and after she peed, slipped the soapy washcloth between her legs.

I made my rounds from patient to patient. If the woman was bedridden, she was rolled onto one side. A grey metal bedpan was wedged under her bare bottom, then she was rolled back over and up onto the pan. I hoisted one after another onto bedpans, waited to hear the tinkle or grunts, and gave them toilet paper or wiped them myself. Then scrubbed their soiled bodies.

One of mine was Mrs. L., the only patient well-to-do enough to have a single room. The day staff dressed her in impeccable suits and a hairdresser kept her hair coiffed, all paid by the family who never came to see her. I started her bedtime routine by turning her wheelchair toward me. Without a word, she whipped out her hidden dinner fork from under a tartan lap blanket and stabbed the back of my hand, guerilla style. That little old lady who didn't know where she was came down hard enough to make blood flow from the puncture of several tines. That was the last night I drug home from that job, put my smelly yellow uniform in a soapy bucket overnight, and started my homework.

Mine was the same job my mother did for seventeen years at the state mental hospital. That's why it seemed such a good find when the nursing home hired me. In the end, it did pay off, because that job taught me what an unskilled worker could expect to do for a lifetime. Thankless, servile, dirty work that paid a pittance. That was not the doing-well life Mr. Berman told me to pursue, the one the Milligans modeled for me, and not the one I was going to accept. I wanted something better. How to get it, I didn't know, but I was determined to find out.

My fellow honors students talked endlessly about going to college. All of them were going, it seemed. Wanted to go. Had to go, according to their families. My goal had been to graduate high school like my brothers did. They finished school, my parents said, proud the boys had gone further than Daddy's sixth grade and Mama's ninth. But my white classmates were going further. They debated the merits of places I'd never heard of, like the University of Rochester or Barnard. Jackie's heart was set on the University of Michigan, where her dad had gone. She had some crazy, foregone conclusion I was going to college too.

I asked my trigonometry teacher, an older woman in lace-up shoes who had encouraged my work, if she thought I should go.

"Why, yes," she said, "a good student like you should apply. I'll set up an appointment for you with the guidance counselor to figure out a plan. She helps on all college questions."

I arrived early to the appointment in my good plaid wrap-around skirt and white blouse to make an impression and browsed college catalogs while waiting my turn.

Then a trim white woman in black heels called me to take the seat she gestured at. She sat behind a desk, empty except for office supplies and a phone book.

"What can I do for you?" the thirty-something Miss Guidance asked.

I bumbled through my request for help figuring out about going to college.

"College?" she asked, raising her eyebrows. "Oh no, Dolores. Colored girls don't go to college. If you do anything after high school, you should go to Fosdick Masten Vocational School and take up sewing. It's right downtown by the baseball stadium."

She flipped her dark hair back over her ear, as white women do to signal what they think is their allure or power, crossed her legs, and rifled through the phone book. She wrote the phone number of the trade school on a slip of paper and handed it to me. Standing up, she went over and opened the office door, signaling the end of the conversation. Not knowing what to say, I thanked her and wandered out, defeated.

Was that why I didn't know about college? I wasn't supposed to go because I was black? But she'd said something ridiculous about me sewing. I'd earned a single D in eleven years of school—in sewing. That D was generous given the skirt I tried to make in eighth-grade home economics with the cheap, stretchy plaid fabric and difficult pleated pattern. That teacher made me take the skirt out and do it over so many times, the final eyesore had uneven pleat widths and plaid lines as wavy as fields of grain. I still wasn't over the humiliation of walking across the auditorium stage in it at the fashion show, before dumping it in the garbage.

Too upset with the counselor's advice to face the kids on the Ghetto Express, I went around to the empty street behind Bennett to think, where nobody would see me.

She hadn't even reviewed my transcript. Was she crazy, randomly picking sewing of all things, out of a hat? None of the white honors students were being told to take up sewing at Fosdick Masten. Pacing up and down the street, I snorted out loud, imagining the eye doctor's cashmere-clad white daughter taking up other people's hems. She would never sit in her fancy mansion with the music room and library I'd seen, pumping the pedal on a Singer sewing machine for a dollar. Why should I?

As I kicked through red and yellow fallen leaves, my rage boiled. I was not about to let this white woman blow me off because I was black. Not after all those firehoses turned on civil rights demonstrators. Not after that new law for equal access Mr. M. kept talking about. I pulled out the notepaper with the phone number to call and ripped it to pieces. I wanted what my white classmates were going to get. That sorry white lady wasn't going to keep me from having it.

Now I wonder how many other worthy students' professional careers that woman killed because of their color. How many lives were consigned to low wages, limited housing, or health choices by other guidance counselors like her? How many teachers, homeowners, dentists, and business leaders were lost to the black community because of them?

I applied blindly to a few colleges in New York state my classmates talked about, without understanding that different colleges taught different things, without knowing the distinction between public and private universities, liberal arts or professional majors. I had no idea some were harder to get into, or which offered scholarships, or what the relevant selection criteria was. I never asked anyone else how to get into college.

Daddy watched me work on applications at the kitchen table as he rinsed collard greens in the sink for Sunday's dinner. "You know college costs a lot of money?" he asked.

I didn't.

"Why are you filling out all those papers? We don't have that kind of extra, you understand? If you want to go to college, I don't know how you're going to pay for it."

I kept on mailing completed applications, adding requests for financial aid, like some of the white kids were doing.

One crisp Saturday morning that fall, Mama and I hung sheets out on the line in the back yard. Our next-door neighbor, Mrs. Mosby, leaned over the chain-link fence and asked if I was taking the exam for Howard University the next Saturday.

Mama and I looked blankly at each other, dropping the wet sheet and wooden clothespins back in the basket to listen. Mrs. Mosby said the scholarship exam could be a great chance to get college paid for, and I should have a good shot at it with my school record. It would be held in the Urban League office where she worked. That neighbor said that education was the way up and out. "You would do well to go to Howard," she said. "It's the leading black university in America."

I'd never heard of it.

"Put her name down," Mama said. "What time will it be?"

The only preparation I made that week was to get the specified pencils and pack a good eraser. It would probably be something like the SAT, which I also hadn't known people prepared for. That Saturday at the Urban League, I answered everything and checked it twice.

Acceptances started coming in for my classmates, including Jackie, who was heading to the University of Michigan. A few mainstream white schools accepted me, like Russell Sage, offering financial aid so paltry Daddy said we'd have to go to the poor house.

I came home from school one afternoon to find Mama still hadn't left for work yet, even though her clock-in time had passed. She sat in the living room in her spotless white shoes, stockings, and nurses' aide uniform, ready for her second shift at the hospital. An oversized envelope rested in her lap, torn open.

"It's all set," she said, beaming. "You did it."

"Did what?"

"You got into Howard University."

"I did? I got in?"

"And, you got a full scholarship. The whole kit and caboodle paid for four years."

"For real, Mama?"

"Yep," she said, handing me the letter on university letterhead that read, "We are pleased to inform you . . ."

I clutched the page, jumping up and down. I *was* going to college. And not just any college, but the most prestigious black university in America. Mama got up from the easy chair and started singing. There was no greater joy, as I clapped in time to her off-key song:

> *Hooray and hallelujah,*
> *You had it comin' to ya.*
> *Goodie, goodie for you,*
> *Goodie, goodie for me.*
> *You rascal, you!*

8

I AM SOMEBODY

It wasn't just my ghetto upbringing I worried could make the Lewises and I unable to relate. It was how my higher education transformed me. Maybe they'll find me uppity. I consider holding back some of my story to see if we could or wanted to first just come together as people. David said I won't even get that far, since they won't accept any nigger relative, educated or not.

In the fall of 1966, I hurried across campus to Howard University's Crampton Auditorium and took a seat for freshman orientation. This was the start of my journey on the road to the good life, whatever that meant. The president, a warrior from the *Brown v. Board of Education* NAACP strategy team, welcomed our all black and brown class from everywhere in the diaspora, calling us the future of the race. We had been admitted, he said, in order to help raise our race. We, the talented tenth, would become all we could be, and lead our people's progress. His message was as electrifying as the fact that he, the distinguished university president, was also black. So were the deans and administrators. It amazed me to see that black people could hold such lofty positions.

In the girl's scholarship dorm, we buckled down, studying pharmacy, mathematics, and economics until the time we lived for came: Saturday night dances at the university ballroom. A girl down the hall had convinced me that "to be seen" at the dances I needed the sophisticated black-is-beautiful Afro of a Howard woman. The campus was leaning into Afrocentric everything. Girls wore kente cloth wrap skirts as we greeted each other in Swahili. *Jambo! Habari gani?* The school of social work was focused on the particular needs of the black community such as poverty and poor education, and the medical school was the center of research on sickle cell anemia, which afflicted mainly African Americans.

A dormmate criticized girls on the floor who straightened the natural curl and kink out of their hair as wanting to be like white people. It wasn't done at Howard, that kind of self-hating denial of your own gene pool. Trying to suppress the "good hair" spawned by my white mother, I sat on the floor between my friend's knees as she rubbed alcohol-soaked cotton onto my roots and strands. My hair kinked more and blew up in volume to something worthier of hep black women. Then I hurried across campus, to show my blacker stuff in the elbow-to-armpit ballroom dance.

So began my growth as a self-aware, proud black person, the hallmark of Howard's black mecca education. Kinky hair was a statement that bolstered my place among the young, gifted, and black, and helped free my mind from the ghetto grids that had nearly limited me.

David did just the opposite in high school. Before he became a Righteous Black Brotha after Vietnam, he'd conked his soft hair. He worked a putrid chemical paste into his roots over the basement laundry tub until its burn made him holler and wash it out. But he was mighty pleased when he ran his hand over his patent leather straight hair, like he was one of the Temptations.

When I look back years later at our efforts to transform our hair, I see how confused we both were. We had not yet discovered how to love who we were as we were, because we wanted so badly to fit in with what black people with other kinds of hair were doing. David wanted conked white hair and I wanted black Afro hair. Our in-between hair was one of those constant reminders that while we said we were black, our biology showed we were mixed. Without the confidence to own what we were, we tried to ignore or downplay that fact around our black brethren.

By the end of my freshman year in 1967, I'd become a Howard Woman—connected, committed, and centered in the black world. It was fabulous, knowing my future was in my black community's rising strength. I gladly inhabited that insular world, building the courage and skills neither I nor my family had had in my earlier upbringing. We knew who we were at Howard, and none of us had any intention of letting white people push us aside when we graduated.

In June 1967, I walked across Howard's main quad in my red-and-white sorority hat, a confident class officer on the dean's list. Out on that wide walkway I ran into a boy I knew vaguely. With a toothy smile, he stuck out his hand and shook mine vigorously, laughing his head off.

"Congratulations," he said.

"Congratulations for what?"

"Didn't you hear? You're not a bastard anymore."

"What are you talking about? I was born legit," I said, pulling my hand away.

He said no, I wasn't, not according to a bunch of states. I had been a bastard all my life, until that day. The US Supreme Court had handed down a decision to overturn anti–race mixing laws still on the state books.

"Used to be against the law in thirty, forty states at one time," he said. "But now all you high-yellas are legal."

Was he saying my parents' marriage was illegal? I thought that was only true down south in the hard-core segregation of Alabama or Mississippi.

"Thanks for the news flash," I said, turning away from him and heading straight over to Founders' Library. Up the wide center stairs and past the research desk, I went to the reading room and pulled the day's *New York Times* off the rack. I wanted to see for myself if this fool was even telling the truth. I stood in the middle of the floor with the newspaper pages spread wide and read the report. A white man and a black woman named Loving had been run out of the state of Virginia for the crime of being married. Instead of spending a year in jail, they could leave the state if they didn't come back for twenty-five years. They sued in a District of Columbia court to be rightfully married in Virginia. The *Times* declared history had been made and another part of America's segregated past abolished when the Supreme Court decided in their favor. Now any race could marry whomever they wanted.

I sat at one of the long wooden study tables to look the paper over again. What white supremacists dreamed up such a law in the first place? Somebody out to protect their racial purity, that's who. During the Loving controversy, some southerners called race-mixing unnatural and an abomination. They were talking about my family. They were talking about me.

Had people seen me as illegitimate all my life and I didn't know it? Or looked at my parents the same way, even though they were legally married in New York State? I checked the article to see if New York law was involved in the ruling. It wasn't. It was a relief that my parents never had to go through anything like the Lovings, being run out of town for being married. I sat in a chair looking out over the sunny quad, not wanting to talk about this with anybody. I was already tired of this whole antimiscegenation business and didn't want to hear it, even if it had just made headline news.

———————

The chair of Howard's economics department, a renowned champion of inner-city economic development, nominated me for a summer Rockefeller Foundation grant at Cornell University the summer before my senior year. Ten of us economics majors from Historically Black Colleges and Universities (HBCUs) were selected for a program designed to proselytize us to apply for Cornell's economics PhD in the fall. But the overwhelmingly complex math in that program turned me off. A black Cornell grad student was sent to convince me.

"I can't do this, man," I told him. "I don't like it at all."

He asked what my minor was and whether I liked it. It was business, and I did like it. "You want to do that?"

"I want to make some money, and move on up, you understand," I said. "Not spend six more years in school."

"Then you want a master's degree in business, an MBA. People are raking up with those credentials. If you go for it, go big. Harvard's the best one."

Thanks to Howard's foundation, I did go on to Harvard Business School, on a full fellowship. The day the acceptance letter came, I danced my happy dance by the bank of dorm mailboxes while other students cheered. The citadel of American power and profit was going to take me straight up the ladder to my dreams.

I graduated from Howard in May 1970. Thousands of families were seated on the grassy quad in brilliant sunshine. We celebrated the 103rd graduation of the university that was established in 1867 to educate newly freed blacks. In that procession were more black doctors, lawyers, engineers, and PhDs graduating than anywhere else in America. In my cap and gown, I bounced gaily with my friends past the audience to our seats. I caught a glimpse of my parents to the right, Mama on the aisle and Daddy bent down next to her, sneaking a taste from his flask.

Jesse Jackson took the podium to give the commencement address. I'd seen him a year or two before, rousing the black crowd down at the massive tent city pitched on the Washington, DC, mall. He was yelling, "Keep Hope Alive!" at the Poor People's Crusade. That live-in was a demonstration to influence government action for more jobs, fair wages, a chance to get out of poverty. I'd been proud to be in the number, honor bound to get a dose of the struggle firsthand.

I hadn't been old enough to go to southern demonstrations in earlier years. But I did sit in an empty classroom with Stokely Carmichael during my Howard years as he urged me to join the Student Non-Violent Coordinating Committee (SNCC) in Mississippi to register voters during Freedom Summers. While I was too scared to risk the bigots putting me in prison or killing me down there, the black power movement and Afrocentrism Howard had imprinted me with the race pride and uplift responsibility that has driven my activism ever since.

As Jesse Jackson warmed up that graduation crowd like the black Baptist minister he was, he used his ready Can-I-just-be-at-home-with-you-friends-and-speak-my-mind? approach. His message wasn't about following our dreams, like white graduates were hearing, although there was some of that. No, I got the life coaching us blacks uniquely needed to survive in white America.

I loved how Jesse told us in his charismatic, poetic cadence to raise ourselves up. "I was born in a slum, but the slum wasn't born in me." He stood in the blazing DC heat in his black honorary doctorate regalia and put his arm in the air in the black power salute. He told us newly minted degree holders and our guests to stand and chant with him, "I Am Somebody."

Some of the audience responded with a polite singsong recitation, like reciting a random slogan off some commercial. People looked at each other, half smiling, humoring him. The truth was, in 1970, black people weren't entirely sure they were somebody. But Jesse insisted, thrusting his fist up hard above his head. Sweat rolled down his face. The crowd's response grew and grew, finally into an outcry that took off into a pulsing roar of sweating, hoping, wanting black people. The pumping fists rose and fell in forceful rhythm with the ululating chant. I was euphoric, realizing Howard *had* turned me into somebody.

The first day at Harvard, I took a seat in the amphitheater classroom designed to foster student debate. Of the ninety classmates who would have all our classes in that same room together the first year, I was one of only four blacks and three women. My confidence fell away as I overheard older white students extol their corporate experience, bandying business concepts about that I'd never heard of. I wondered how I got in.

My largely entitled, aggressive, and impressively smart classmates, including an Argentine aristocrat and sons of major American corporate presidents, had a lively discussion on what a good EPS was. I leaned over ask my neighbor what EPS was. As he told me "earnings per share," the look on his face was quizzical, like "How couldn't you know something that simple?" I felt like the same isolated black kid on my first day of high school honors classes. Sweating it among confident white people who believed it their due to belong there but thought I didn't became my life.

Some white 44-Long student I didn't know came around the curved corridor of Aldrich Hall and physically blocked me moving to my next class. That well-built preppy wanted me to know I had no business being there. What was Harvard thinking, he demanded, giving his highly qualified friend's seat to me and rejecting the friend? Affirmative action had no place at Harvard, and I was going to waste the education. He walked off as abruptly as he'd confronted me, not waiting for a reply.

His outburst made me doubt the opportunity I had, not because I couldn't learn what the business school taught, but because it gave me a glimpse of the personal price of dealing with that kind of attitude in business. It stressed me more to wonder if it would be worth it or if I should run while I had the chance.

A couple days later, a professor called on me to discuss a case on the prospects for a new type of washing machine. I tried to equate the number of loads Mama and I had gotten done over our basement washtubs against the new, improved machines that Company A planned to revolutionize the market with. After presenting my opening analysis, discussion was thrown open for comment. The class ate me alive. About forty students, intent on squeezing out more profit, not clean clothes, waved their hands and jumped out of their seats to win points by trashing my arguments. Their surprising aggression, something I had never seen in a classroom, rendered me unable to rebut. Some behavior was more one-upmanship than worthwhile contributions, just as I came to understand when working in corporations. It was part of the game. Be seen. Be dominant. Put the other guy down so you can get ahead. As classes went on, some students who even made ridiculous comments were entertained. One suggested putting police in pink uniforms to diffuse civic tensions. The aristocrat suggested financing a New York subway expansion by raising fares to twenty-five dollars.

The first six weeks ground me down. I wondered if I did fit, sitting quietly back in my third-row seat, observing the fray. Classmates with three to seven years of business experience, as well as military officers and corporate managers, eagerly dove into that shark tank, harpooning each other with concepts I had yet to learn. I realized there was much more to this program than solving cases every night on how to design factories and create strategies to improve balance sheets. There were major deficits to overcome.

Perhaps the youngest person admitted out of a class of nine hundred, straight out of undergrad, one of only a couple dozen blacks, and without any business experience whatever, I became progressively more depressed. The white kids were having parties to which the blacks were not invited. There was no concerned black faculty to talk with as there had been at Howard.

With the first marking period, we black students compared notes and found that the same accounting professor gave every one of us a grade of "low pass." It had been a silly dream, thinking all it took to get a degree from Harvard was hard work. With no counselors or support to turn to, I decided to quit.

I left my partly filled suitcase in the middle of the dorm room floor and went to the dining hall for dinner. It was the final minutes the hall was open, when hopefully all the students had gone. As I slid my tray down the steam-table rail, the lone black employee on campus, a dark stout woman in an apron and hairnet, waited. I dithered disinterestedly over the choices.

"What's the matter tonight?" she asked. "How you feel?"

"OK, I guess." Why tell her anything? She'd never understand.

"You keep your head up, hear? Don't you let nobody, and nothing, stop you."

She defiantly put both a piece of beef and a piece of chicken on my plate, her own expression of support.

"I'm rootin' for you. Awlright?" Her stare was the tough love look my grandmother cast over us, her kind of encouragement, telling us what was expected while making clear what we had better do.

I nodded at the cafeteria lady and thanked her. My grandmother had given me $2,000 of her remaining $5,000 life savings to go to Harvard. These older black people put their hopes for the race in people like me, just as Howard University had.

Harvard had let me in and claimed they made no admissions mistakes. I went back to my room and put my sweaters back in the drawer. Across the hall, I told the two black guys rooming together that I'd thought of quitting. They laughed like Richard Pryor had delivered the punch line in a new stand-up act.

"Fool," one said, "we're all struggling. But ain't none of us quitting. Not us and not you." We talked for hours about our frustrations and what it took to succeed, even if the whites had shut us out of their study groups and never invited us to their parties. Those two men became lifelong brothers to me.

In the next two years, the notion that being educated meant the polite recitation of facts or correct calculations evaporated. Day after day we ground through complex business case studies, sharpening the analytical arguments and decisions that could cost or make hundreds of millions of dollars. It seemed like Monopoly money at first, yet in our daily cases, we were taught that we would be the people making those decisions in our careers. It was like nothing I'd ever thought of, and certainly nothing I'd ever heard black people talk about.

I was uncomfortable with my weak presentations. Other students who were born to leadership, like the heir to a dairy fortune or the son of the president of a major luggage company, were smooth and poised. I took notes on the polished code of the executive suite flowing out of their mouths, their casual mastery of the game.

That was a critical part of where I wanted to go. My success would depend on me coming to the conference table with solidly analyzed ideas, convincingly delivered in business protocol. Even if you can read music, you can't have the solo if you can't sing. I quit marveling and got in the mirror, practicing the prescribed code of my business-savvy classmates: "Cut the level three features and price as a loss leader so we can beat the competition to market." I'd come too far not to play the game that would get me out of my old less-than life.

Two years later, I walked behind top-hatted marshals in the graduation procession at Harvard's outdoor Tercentenary Theatre. The tinny sound of the student orchestra wafted over us. I caught a glimpse of the day's speaker, Aleksandr Solzhenitsyn, the writer who exposed Russia's forced labor camps and gulags.

The throng of guests we filed past captivated me. Hundreds of America's elite were assembled in that campus audience. They were the white parents and families of my jeans-and-sneakered classmates who, save my Jewish roommate, had never invited me to anything in our two years together. I saw their self-assurance, tanned and dressed in custom clothes, especially the athletically built white man in a pale lemon sports jacket with gold trimmed heels on his shoes. He chatted in modulated pleasantries through thin lips and straight white teeth, tilting his salt-and-pepper head toward his elegant wife.

Sitting among them, the program went on as printed, though not much of what was said and done that day stays with me now. My mind was somewhere else, thinking about where I came from and where I was going. Howard had taught me I was somebody who had a chance. Harvard had taught me I should expect success managing major businesses.

That sunny morning of grandeur was my graduation from so much more than Harvard. I'd earned my ticket out of the ghetto and into a life with the same choices white people had. Or so it seemed.

What I remember most about that day was thinking about my high school guidance counselor. The one who flipped that black hair behind her ear and wrote the sewing school phone number for me, because "colored girls don't go to college."

If only she could see me now, I thought, the colored girl that impeached her null-and-void, past-its-expiration-date, bankrupt guidance.

9

SEARCHING

The clerk in the polyester dress at Vital Records in the Marion County, Indiana, courthouse handed some forms over the counter. "Fill these out, one for each person you're looking for," she said without looking up.

I only had five days to find Mama's family before getting back to New Jersey. Earlier that morning, I'd read through the yellowing pages of annual city directories at the main library, starting with the year Mama left, 1943. My grandparents, Henry and Mildred Lewis, were listed right there, the first place I looked. A tinge of some connection to these relatives was short lived, as Mildred's name disappeared four years later, and Henry's in six, in 1949. There was no sister Dorothy listed at all.

Now, I cooled my heels at the Vital Records Office until the clerk said there was no documentation on Mildred. There were only spotty records kept back then, she explained. Mildred must have died of consumption in 1947, like Mama predicted.

But the clerk did have Henry Lewis's death certificate. My grandfather was dead? But Mama expected him to be alive, and so I had too. In fact, Mama had told me to look him over good and tell her exactly how he was doing. And though I hadn't considered it, he had died of a heart attack in 1949, thirty years before I got to Indy.

I leaned against a wall. So, I wouldn't be able to look for familiar features in my grandfather's face, or search his eyes for the goodness in his soul? I'd never find out what he'd say about Mama's marriage? Or whether he'd receive me as his own?

The end of the search for my grandparents was over before lunchtime on the first day. Maybe this was a fool's errand, to think I could find the other half of my family, those whose blood ran in my veins. I never knew them. Now I never would.

The smell of somebody's menthol cigarette wafted over me. Delicious Kool Filters, like I used to smoke. I inhaled that lovely secondhand smoke for a moment. It was the only comfort available in that moment, so I paused to float there because I didn't know what to do next.

I went to Mama's old house at 635 Woodlawn Avenue in the morning. Maybe Dorothy was still there. If not, somebody else might remember the family. Using directions from the hotel desk clerk, the old quiet neighborhood of modest single-family houses was easy to find. I searched Woodlawn Avenue to find number 635, with the front porch where Mama had entertained callers.

There was no such address. Where her house should have been was only broken sidewalks fronting an empty lot and a few unkempt city trees. The neighbor's house across the street with the four daughters all named Mary was gone like the rest. I'd expected to talk with them, to see what they knew. Up at the end of the street it dead-ended in a cement barrier, and a highway ran nearby. Good old urban planning.

St. Patrick's, Mama's Catholic parish, was just a few blocks away. The genealogy class emphasized using the marriage, funeral, and baptism records kept by houses of worship. But the main door, which Mama must have gone through for mass every Sunday, was locked. So was the back. At the adjacent stone rectory, no priest in a cassock or housekeeper in an apron answered the bell either. I called back later and left a message requesting a search for Lewis family records.

The only person left to look for was Dorothy. Figuring she must have married I went down to the basement of the Marion County records office to search for her license. At a small wooden table, I read through handwritten ledgers with every bride's name from 1943 to 1953. No Dorothy.

Maybe she never did get married. She would have been an old maid by then, at thirty-four. Or maybe she married outside Marion County. How the devil was I supposed to figure out all the marriage records in Indiana, or the whole United States? There was no telling where she could be.

She might still be in town under her maiden name. The next day, using the entire set of phone books borrowed from the front desk, I called every permutation of her name I could think of. Men, women, and children answered, young sounding, country sounding, annoyed sounding people. Some were wrong numbers, disconnected numbers, or answering machines. None of them were my aunt.

On my last night I sat in the chair by my hotel window with the lights turned off, looking out at Indianapolis. Was she out there somewhere? I scanned the horizon dully, out of ideas. My family search had gone nowhere—no grandparents, no aunt, no house, no neighbors, no priest. No family. And I had to get back to New Jersey in the morning. A sob burst out of me. My lungs heaved to refill. In defeat, I cried, much too loudly for a hotel room.

As was my habit, I went to the airport way ahead of time. While waiting at the gate, all the steps of my week's search ran through my mind. That priest had never called back. What was his deal anyway, when I'd mentioned how important the church records were to me? I decided to call him one more time to see if anything had turned up. Not that he'd answer. In the phone booth across from the gate, I juggled my briefcase and purse on my lap, got a piece of paper and a pen at the ready, then dialed.

The good father answered. He'd found my aunt's marriage recorded at St. Patrick's in 1944. Apparently, the marriage license clerk hadn't recorded everybody's nuptials downtown. Dorothy Lewis had married a soldier stationed in California during WWII.

"Do you have his name?"

"Name of Anthony Boehle."

"Can you spell that, please?"

"B-o-e-h-l-e. BO-LEE, I think you'd say. That's all we've got. No address."

"Thank you so much. This is great."

"You're welcome. Good luck finding her. Now, don't forget to send us a donation."

I hung up and pulled the directory that hung from a chain beneath the phone up onto the metal counter. Paging under the Bs, I found Anthony Boehle, the only Boehle in the book.

I put change in the phone and dialed immediately. The noise in the busy airport was so loud I cupped my hand over the receiver. The phone rang four times.

A lady answered.

"Is this Mrs. Anthony Bo-lee?"

"Yes," she answered. Her heavy voice was put-upon, the kind people use for solicitations.

"Well, you don't know me, but I think we might be related. Would you mind answering some questions to see if you are the person I'm looking for?" I asked.

"Uh, OK, I'll answer a few."

"You grew up at 635 Woodlawn Avenue in Indianapolis?"

"Yes." Her voice became guarded.

"Your family attended St. Patrick's Catholic Church?"

"Yes, yes we did."

"Your father was named Henry Lewis?"

"Yes."

I stood up in the booth, excited now, but trying not to rush, not to scare her off.

"He was an electrician?"

"Yes, he was," she said slowly.

"He worked on the first lighting system at the Indianapolis 500 Speedway?"

"Yes."

I paused, to get the next part right.

"You had a sister who disappeared in the early 1940s?"

A chair scraped the floor on her end. Silence, then, "Yes."

"Her name was Merna Elizabeth."

"Uh, no. That wasn't my sister's name."

We were both quiet. How to clarify what made no sense? She had to be the one, but what else could I say? I stared across the flow of passengers in the concourse. My fellow travelers were milling about, ready to begin boarding. There wasn't much time.

I started over with Mrs. Boehle, double-checking the same questions about her father's name, occupation, address.

She replied yes to all of them over again. "That's right. Yes, yes."

"Your name is Dorothy Lewis Boehle, right?"

"It is." Then I was back to my mother's name.

"Your sister was called Ella?" I asked her. That was Mama's nickname, the one I thought Daddy had given her.

"Yes, oh yes, that was my sister. Ella Lewis," she said.

"Her given name was Merna Elizabeth, right?"

"I don't know that name. She was always Ella to us. Now tell me. *Who* are you?" Her anxiety colored every word.

"I am Ella's daughter."

"Ella's daughter? You are Ella's daughter?"

"Yes, I am your sister's daughter. I've been in Indianapolis for a week looking for you, uh, my family." I was excited but held my tongue, waiting.

"Oh, my Lord! Ella's daughter? How can that be? We thought she must be dead."

"I realize this comes as a shock after so many years, but yes, I can assure you I am Ella Lewis's daughter, the youngest of her three children."

"She was married and had three children?"

"Yes, she was."

"Where has she been all this time?"

"Buffalo. We were raised in Buffalo, New York."

"Buffalo? We never knew she was in Buffalo. After she left Indy, we never heard from her again."

"Yes, I know. But I'm reaching out to you now, hoping to meet you if you are willing, after all these years. Are you?"

"Where are you now? Still in Indy?"

"Yes, at the airport, about to catch a flight home." As I looked over at the gate again, unbelievably, the agent posted a two-hour delay on the departure board. Relief rushed through me. I wouldn't have to go home only imagining who my white people were. We'd have time to talk, if they didn't reject my race right off. I just wanted to see what their background was with my own eyes. Because of the way my parents ran to get married, and the fear of trouble if her family knew, I had no expectations beyond just saying hello. "It takes off in two hours," was all I got out before Dorothy cut in.

"Stay there. I'm coming out to you now. I want to meet you too."

"You do? Good, I'll wait for you. I'm heavyset, with glasses."

She hung up without telling me how she looked. Neither of us had thought to say what airline, what flight, or what gate we'd meet at. Stuck to the phone booth seat, I closed my eyes to picture the sweet-faced eighteen-year-old girl in the only photo of Dorothy Mama had. She was slender, standing in their yard in a full-length dress for some occasion.

The first man in line to use the phone knocked on the glass and jerked his head to the side. I moved to a wall across from my gate, to search the faces of older white women. For the next forty-five minutes, none of the swarm of people who flowed by or waited for friends and families were for me. Then I a spotted a gray-haired, stout white woman dressed in pastel pants like Mama would wear. She stumbled toward me from way down the concourse, moving intently toward my crowded gate. With her eyes glued on mine, she staggered up to me.

"It's you, isn't it?" She studied my features like a mother with her newborn. "I see my sister in your face," she said.

That old prickling cold shocked my back, like in all my most anxious moments. When my back froze, I lost the ability to respond in critical situations. And here I couldn't speak either. She kept peering at me, confident in her identification. Nobody had ever said I looked like Mama. But she saw it. It was her all right. Had to be.

She didn't share any of Mama's features, and all resemblance to the photo when she was slim and fresh-faced was gone. She was heavy, while

Mama was thin. But they were half sisters, something I had forgotten when imagining her looks. The one thing she did share with Mama and me was height, at around five foot one.

"Yes, I'm Dolores Johnson," I finally managed. "Ella Lewis's daughter." I extended my hand and put a pleasant expression on my face as we shook formally, the way I did business colleagues. "Good to meet you."

She gestured to her husband, Tony, a short, no-nonsense looking man with gray hair. He stood back from her, watching me. Tony removed the pipe from his mouth and shook my hand.

"Hello," he said. I'd have some explaining to do to satisfy a man with sharp eyes like his.

Everything in that crowded, noisy airport disappeared except for this unassuming, working-class white aunt and uncle. So, this was who my white family was.

Dorothy talked fast. "You gave me the shock of my life. I left the meal half cooked and rushed straight out here. I had to meet you, but now that we're here, I hardly know what to say."

"That's two of us," I said. We got a table in the coffee shop where we could talk.

We stirred our coffee, each staring into the steaming dark wells of our confusion in a pregnant silence. I'd been so intent on the search to just find these people I hadn't given an iota of thought to what to say if I found them.

Dorothy looked up first. "You must know we all thought Ella died in the '40s. Your showing up is absolutely unbelievable. Why, to think she got married and had a family, and didn't let us know. What I don't understand is why would my sister have run away from her family without a word all these years?"

I kept her gaze and just laid it out. "She married a Negro. Somebody you didn't know. Back then, 1943, was a time when race mixing wasn't allowed in Indiana."

I barreled on to get the story out before they said anything. "She thought the family wouldn't accept it and would suffer for her decision." They stared at me with incomprehension.

"Like your dad wouldn't get work, the family might be shunned, even that your marriage prospects would be hurt."

Tony grunted, watching me closely. Did he believe me? Or maybe he was considering whether he'd have married Dorothy if he'd known her sister was married to a black man.

"See," I said, "she didn't want to ruin your lives. She didn't want to leave you either, but it was dangerous for my dad to be with a white woman in Indiana and illegal for them to intermarry."

"Illegal?"

Dorothy was apparently as ignorant of the laws when it came to "Negro business" as Mama had been. After what happened in my life, I found it incomprehensible that she was that removed from what we black people had gone through.

"So, as painful as it was," I said, "my mother thought it best for all of you if you never knew what she did or where she went."

Dorothy and Tony went back to stirring their coffee again. I braced for them to get up and walk out, scandalized or disgusted with what my mother had done. I half expected them to say something ugly and racist like David had predicted, or to reject me personally. I was ready. Plenty of white folks had already toughened me up.

I'd only wanted to see them. Find out if they existed. Know what type of people they were. Mission accomplished. I studied both their downturned faces, trying to read their reaction.

After what seemed like forever, Dorothy said, "She was probably right. Mother especially. She would turn in her grave."

Tony kept his head bowed.

I opened my wallet to the family photo I carried. They held it up close to see the five of us together, taken on the day Charles Nathan graduated high school in his black gown and I graduated eighth grade in my white crinoline dress. I pointed out Mama, Daddy, my brothers, and myself, giving our ages.

"Well, I'll be." Dorothy leaned into her husband. "That's my sister. That is Ella." She looked into Tony's eyes, and he nodded. "Look how beautiful she is here with her family." Her eyes flashed and she scooted closer to me. "Where is my sister now?"

I put on as sincere a face as I could before saying Mama had passed away. My back tingled as the bald-faced lie slipped through my lips. Here I was trying to relate to people I'd gone to all this trouble to meet and was ruining my chances with Mama's deception. But what else could I do? A waitress bumped the back of my chair as she hoisted a tray of drinks, breaking into my dithering conscience. My loyalty was to my mother, and she'd made me promise. I rationalized that I didn't even know this lady.

"Dead?" Dorothy cried. "Ella's dead? How did she die?"

I hadn't thought ahead about any explanations. I searched for more lies to make this trusting soul believe. My tingles turned to ice.

"Well, she had a sudden heart attack," I mumbled, "and died on the spot."

"When, when did my sister die?"

"Two years ago. She's buried in Buffalo," I said, wondering if it sounded true.

"To think we missed all those years of being together," she said. "Only to find out too late she's already gone." Her shoulders slumped. She spoke so softly I could hardly hear her amid all the conversation at tables around us. "What I would have given to see her again."

Was she saying she was OK with Mama marrying a black man? That she loved Mama even now? That had to be her meaning, if she wanted to see Mama again. My mind was blown; I couldn't put an answer together.

She said the last communication from Ella was a postcard from New York the week after she left to visit a friend in Massachusetts. When they didn't hear from her, they got worried.

"Dad scraped together the money and went to New York to search in the last place she was ever heard from. The police opened a missing person's case and they searched ever' where, in Indianapolis and New York. But they couldn't find any trace of her, and her body was never found. The police declared her a victim of foul play."

"How awful for all of you," I said, thinking how Mama would cry to know they suffered so trying to find her.

"It surely was. Dad never got over it. She was his favorite, you know."

I'd expected to defend myself against a racist, but instead here I was teary eyed over these people's pain, my own relative's pain. Everybody had suffered, in both Indiana and Buffalo. I'd been so shortsighted about stirring this pot I hadn't imagined how it could burn those involved. Dorothy was as stunned now as Mama had been when I said I wanted to search for her family. So now I was responsible for Dorothy's feelings too, even as I told her one lie after another. Why hadn't I thought this through?

Dorothy brought out a photo of her four daughters, born in the same time as my brothers and me. All of them were in Indianapolis except one who lived in Florida with her family. Dorothy confirmed that her dad died in 1949 and her mother in 1947 from consumption.

We talked about how both the sisters had been nurses' aides, just as I had, how Daddy was a welder and Tony had worked at a GM factory. How the sisters had lived similar blue-collar, middle-class lives and raised families in the same years without ever knowing it.

As I readied to board the plane, I asked if they wanted to exchange contact information. We did, and agreed to talk again, although neither of us suggested a specific plan. We shook hands good-bye. It wasn't jubilant and it wasn't hostile. We were daunted, two shocked parties, newly related but not knowing what to do about it.

———

When Luther picked me up at Newark Airport, he'd only heard the blow-by-blow each night on the phone, not what happened that final day. He hugged me and said, "I'm so sorry it didn't work out after all the hopes and work you put into it."

I pushed back a bit from him and laughed.

"What?"

"It did work out. Today, I met my aunt at the Indianapolis airport." The day's events tumbled out of me on the drive home, Luther whistling and grunting with every reveal.

We sat together on our brown Naugahyde couch in the den that evening, talking through my highs and lows in Indy. We drank white wine late into that night until I ran out of steam.

Luther asked, "So now, tell me, does all this help you know better who you are?"

The triumph was I got to see Mama's family. But what he asked was bigger: did that clear up the questions about my own identity? How did finding out my white half had lots of people hanging on my tree change my being black? I realized that was as murky as before.

"Honestly, I don't know what this means."

"What now?" Luther asked.

"I don't know. It's just been a few hours. Maybe I'll get back in touch with them someday."

"But how can you, when you've said your mother is dead?"

"Huh?"

"You think they'll trust you when they find out she's not? Those lies cannot stand, and you know it." Luther got into bed, telling me to straighten that out with Mama. "Com' on now, gimme that wing, and let's get some sleep" he said, turning onto his side.

I climbed in with him, wondering if I'd found and then lost Mama's family in a single day by telling that lie. He just might be right.

The next morning, I called Mama to report, with both Daddy and Luther on their respective extensions.

"What happened?" she said with a hint of ready tears. "Did you find them?"

She took the news of Mildred's death with a soft, "Oh, no," then finally said, "None of us thought she would live long back then. Her consumption was bad." All four of us fell quiet while she digested this.

"What about Dad? Did you see him?" Her voice was so anxious.

"No, no. I didn't. I'm so sorry to tell you he died in 1949, thirty years ago."

"Dad's dead? Been dead all those years? Are you sure?" She acted like she'd seen him yesterday and here I was calling to say her father dropped dead last night. She burst out crying.

I read the death certificate in front of me, which listed a heart attack as the cause.

She wanted to know if he'd been sick a long time, and if he suffered. I wished I could tell her more.

"I'm an orphan now," Mama said, her voice like glass shattering.

Children could be orphaned, but hearing a senior citizen say that was puzzling. Apparently, Mama had buried her loving attachment to the younger father she left behind, and now when death suddenly stole him from her, she responded like a child.

Daddy tried to comfort her from his bedroom extension, but then went downstairs and stayed beside her in the kitchen. The whole rest of the call, I could hear him in the background asking her, "What's she saying now, Ella?" Mama would stop talking to me to tell details to him, and then his reactions back to me.

"What about Dorothy?" Mama asked.

"I found her, Mama. I met her."

"Charles, oh, Charles." She was offline again, telling him, "She met her," repeating herself, crying.

Once she quieted, I described having coffee with Dorothy and her husband, Tony, for about an hour, and how they were nice to me. She wanted to know everything.

I explained we were all in shock, sitting at one of those plastic airport tables, trying to understand who each other was. It had been cautious; a polite feeling out of a stranger you had to reveal a life-changing secret to. With each explanation about Dorothy's daughters and her parents' deaths, Mama sifted through the details as if panning for gold.

"Now," Mama asked, "what did you tell Dorothy about me?"

"They know you married a black man. And why you didn't get in touch. They seemed to have understood it some."

"What did she say?"

I said once it sunk in, what her staying in Indy with Daddy would have done to the family, that Dorothy said Mama was probably right. And how Dorothy was sad and disappointed, but not mad. Not mad at all.

"Dorothy wanted to know where you are now," I said.

"Did you say what we agreed on?"

"Yes, I said you were dead, like you told me to. And they believed me."

"So, I don't have to face her?"

"No, you don't. Dorothy thinks you're dead." Then I took my chance and suggested we had to decide what to do next.

"What do you mean, next? You found them, like you said you wanted to. That's IT."

Luther came in the kitchen, sweeping his index finger across his throat.

"I felt bad saying you were dead, telling lies to someone who regretted missing all those years you were alive."

Mama said there wasn't going to be any next step. She was angry, a feeling she so rarely expressed, I didn't reply. She was my mother, after all.

"Look, Dolores, finding Dorothy was a blessing," she whispered. "Something I'll always be grateful to you for. But we agreed you'd say I was dead. I expect you to stick to your word."

"OK, Mama, OK." I hung up, knowing that was the end of it.

10

DEEP SOUTH

Back in 1973, I spent the Fourth of July weekend upstate with my best friend Valerie and her new husband. It felt good to get out of New York City's noise and dirt, where I lived and managed a large call center. They didn't tell me, but her husband had arranged for his best friend to escort me for the long weekend. Luther, a delicious African American gentleman, was like me, a first-generation college graduate with a new master's degree. He was six years older and six inches taller, with a Chevron mustache of thick hair. Smart, fine, and sincere.

After just the first evening, his moon-shaped eyes shimmered in pursuit. He and I stayed up late talking, long after his IBM guys' Friday night poker game ended in my host's rec room. We shared our dreams of climbing the corporate ladder with the right partner at our side, me in marketing and Luther in engineering, where he hoped to be promoted soon.

He came back each day, to teach me to bowl (a ruse to put his hands around my waist), to play badminton with me at an afternoon BBQ, and to show me his moves at a late-night party.

That Monday night, rather than take the bus back to Manhattan as planned, Luther drove me the three hours home. Then he turned around to drive the three hours back so he could get to work the next morning. After that, our romance was a runaway train.

We partied with our best-friends' couple, learned to dance the rock at New York's Copacabana night club, and went to civil rights leader Wyatt T. Walker's Baptist church in Harlem, where talents from Broadway shows played and sang the real, real gospel music.

When the promotion he wanted at IBM didn't come through, Luther applied elsewhere. An attractive offer was made, but it was in South Carolina. Rather than live apart, he asked me to marry him and move down there together. After six months of dating I said yes, and our parents gave us their blessing.

Our decision was still secret at work the night Luther accompanied me to my office party. We sat with my boss on wooden stools, watching the stream of red taillights inching forward on the crowded street outside while the two men made small talk. When the boss asked about his work, Luther said he was moving out of state for a better job and taking me with him. I scrunched my forehead at him, unprepared to tell yet. Not only did the boss enthusiastically congratulate us, he and Luther immediately began strategizing on how to get me a company transfer to the South Carolina office.

We took our vows under a floral arch in the church where I grew up, then moved to Greenville, South Carolina. Despite the beautiful weather and more relaxed southern lifestyle that allowed us newlyweds to sneak out of work and be together for an hour during the day, we were regularly confronted with racist situations. My new management banned me from calling on Bob Jones University because they did not want African Americas on their campus, nor, for that matter, did several other large accounts. The owner of a large car dealership who was my customer motioned for me to sit and wait while he finished a phone call. Putting his hand over the receiver, he winked and whispered, "It's a nigger. You know they can't afford a car." He was only one of many to reveal what whites said about blacks behind our backs because he mistook my identity. Local blacks were reluctant, or maybe afraid, to go with us to a new "white" nightclub where we heard the prime rib was good. A gas station attendant stuck his face in my car window to obnoxiously study my skin and demand to know, "What are you?"

We only stayed in South Carolina long enough for Luther to discover his new job was not a fit. Just long enough to figure out how far "yonder" was and that the supermarket bag boy was talking to my twenty-six-year-old self when he said, "Ma'am." In less than a year, Luther got another offer at a prominent company and I got another company transfer, to Baton Rouge, Louisiana.

However, when we called my parents, jubilant with the news that we both had management jobs and were moving there, they said we'd lost our minds.

Mama said it was a mistake to move that far from family, where we didn't know anybody. Daddy said, "But, it's the Deep South. Not the South, but the Deep South. There's a difference."

"What's the difference?" I asked.

"It's not as safe as South Carolina, or even North Carolina where they desegregated lunch counters without anybody getting killed. You know Louisiana was one of the big plantation states, one of them that never got over losing their slaves. Hell, it is right next to Mississippi. And you know what they did in Mississippi."

Of course, I did. Every black person knew Mississippi was the most lethally racist place in the United States. Medgar Evers and two other black men were murdered because they urged our people to register and vote. Three young volunteers disappeared, and their bodies were found buried in a dam wall one Freedom Summer. And deep-voiced Nina Simone channeled our incredulity and disgust at such hate in her song, "Mississippi Goddamn."

"Don't forget Emmett Till," Daddy said. "It's dangerous, I say dangerous, in the Deep South."

The ghoulish evil of fourteen-year-old Emmett Till's murder in 1955 Mississippi had been captured in a photo printed in *JET*, the black-owned weekly. The boy lay in his open casket, both eyes gouged out, cheeks and temples smashed in, the body swollen from drowning, disfigured nearly beyond human resemblance. He was killed while visiting from Chicago, for supposedly saying something to a white woman. Two accused white men were acquitted by an all-white jury in a sham trial. Later they admitted to killing Emmett when they were beyond the statute of limitations.

"Some of those crackers are still down there," Daddy said.

"Emmett Till was twenty years ago," I said. "It's 1975. Things are different now. We've got the civil rights bills passed. Everything is integrated."

"Well, daughter, since they killed that child, I get on my knees every day and thank God we live in the North."

Luther and I figured Daddy was out of step with the times. We weren't going to Louisiana as uneducated, disenfranchised field workers like Daddy's family had been on a backwoods Georgia farm. They'd fled to Buffalo for a better chance way back in the 1930s and hadn't been back to see what it's like now. And Emmett Till was just a child who grown men could easily take advantage of. Now it was the 1970s and Luther and I both held master's degrees. It was more than a decade since the *New York Times* pronounced the new 1964–65 civil rights laws the death knell of segregation. And since we expected that to be true, we went on and moved to Louisiana. We told Daddy we would watch out for troublemakers, sure, but we would be accepted on the merit of who we were.

Once the moving van was loaded and on its way to Baton Rouge, Luther flew ahead to start his position. I set out driving early in the morning to allow enough sunlight to go straight through the thirteen-hour trip across the South. I was a good enough driver to handle the trip. It was being a young black woman driving alone through former Confederate states that made me nervous. What if the car broke down somewhere in my father's version of the Deep South, leaving me at the mercy of the crackers he said could get me?

I'd prepared to avoid all that. Changed the oil, had the mechanic check the car for road worthiness, bought jumper cables. The TripTik map from AAA was on the front seat with the route highlighted in yellow. My own food was packed so there would be no need to go into a restaurant. And if it got dark and I had to get a room, I had the Negro Motorist Green Book, a guide assembled by black postmen listing places Negroes could sleep or get a meal without trouble.

On my quest to get to Luther as quickly as possible, I drove directly through South Carolina, Georgia, and Alabama. Then, as I neared the border where Alabama meets Mississippi, I filled up my gas tank and went to the bathroom on the Alabama side, and made it my business not to stop for any reason in Mississippi.

When I arrived that same day at Luther's Baton Rouge hotel room, after dark, I don't know which of us was more relieved that I'd made it without incident. We talked a little, and because it was late, he went on to bed while I took my time winding down in the shower.

While hot water beat on my back, the geography I'd sped past rolled by in my mind. It was such a shame not to have stopped along the way to enjoy places in my country I would have loved to see. Across miles and miles of Georgia and Alabama, I'd longed to get out and smell the magnificently laden red, pink, and white azalea bushes and to examine the stately magnolia trees' creamy blossoms and grand old trunks. As road signs announced the way to the storied Tuskegee Institute, founded by Booker T. Washington, I thought how wonderful it would be to see Howard's sister HBCU and check out what a country campus was like. There had to be a museum there showcasing George Washington Carver's many peanut inventions, accomplishments that would have made me proud to learn about. I had slowed down but reluctantly went on past the Tuskegee exit sign. Not too far afterward, a second sign appeared, giving me another chance to see the institute. But no, I told myself, it was best to press on down the interstate as planned.

At a gas stop, I hesitated over the impulse to take the TripTik option to detour onto a longer way through Mississippi, down along the scenic Biloxi and Gulfport beach coast on the Gulf of Mexico. But I didn't make that choice either. Those places probably weren't for me, or any African Americans, even if I stayed in the car and just looked through the window. I wasn't fool enough to risk getting caught in the dark in Mississippi. And the extra time it took might mean being too exhausted to get to Baton Rouge that night. No way would I sleep in Mississippi. So, I plowed on straight to Baton Rouge, missing all the sights that called to me, because I was afraid. As life would have it, there has never been another chance for me to see any of those places.

———————

Luther and I got off to a good start in Baton Rouge, learning the layout of the town with very helpful assistance from the pleasant hotel staff. They pointed out landmarks, marked routes to our jobs on maps, told us how the Louisiana State University (LSU) football games took over the town. And they sent us down the Airline Highway to Ralph & Kacoo's restaurant, where we were made comfortable by the smiling white hostess who welcomed us with chatty charm. That Cajun food was so delicious we went back again and again, each time eating the whole bowl of hot hushpuppies with fried fish from the Mississippi, Atchafalaya crawfish tails in thick étouffée sauce, seafood gumbo, and shrimp stew, but never the alligator bites. The famed southern hospitality we encountered everywhere was so lovely after New York's brusqueness, we questioned what my father had been talking about.

Luther found a black colleague at the plant who also lived in Baton Rouge, and they began carpooling for the forty-five-mile commute. We were invited over to meet his wife and small children, where we were taken in warmly. It felt good to make that early connection, to know somebody black in town we could visit with, and to look forward to others they planned to introduce us to. The easy way we newcomers were welcomed as members of the tribe made the move feel comfortable.

My first day in the company sales office, I wore a sleeveless black-and-white dress and black patent pumps to make a good first impression. There would be the day in the office and later, a management dinner with higher ups from New Orleans and regional management from Birmingham.

My boss, a district manager in his mid-thirties, received me in his corner office. We hadn't met before, so we got acquainted before he discussed my role. Then he took me on a tour of the office, introducing me to the all-white staff. Men in white shirts and ties and a few women in dresses shook my hand as we visited row after row of cubicles. A few offered their help as I settled in. In the break room, there was no way to miss the string bean of a white man in a seersucker suit and white shoes tasting coffee from the fifty-cup metal percolator. He shouted, "Who made this turkey piss?" which I learned was his ritual complaint about needing more chicory.

A tall older man with thinning black hair came to hang over the top of my cubicle. His lugubrious grin conflicted with his beady eyes. They were hard, like a rat caught in the night. "Hey, heard you was here," he started, as lightly as an old friend. "Got a joke for you, heh, heh. What do you call a nigger on a stick?"

"What did you say?"

"A fudgsicle. A nigger on a stick's a fudgsicle. Git it?" He slapped his thigh and walked away laughing.

People around me kept their heads down, working like nothing happened. Should I say something back or ignore an intentional insult? I'd only been on the job a few hours. I kept quiet, wondering what planet I'd landed on.

Later that evening, in a private dining room of a nice restaurant, I was seated near the ranking official from Birmingham at a long banquet table. In what was apparently another southern gesture, he presented a long-stemmed red rose to me and to the other woman attending, with a courtly grace. I'd certainly never seen such from businessmen in New York.

I introduced myself as the new sales manager to colleagues seated to my left.

"Oh my," the other female said, and laughed. She'd tried to get into sales a few years before, the first woman to do so. But she didn't get the job. During the interview, the man in charge told her why.

"What if we had to send a nice lady like you to call on some nigger bar?" she imitated, amused. "He was right," she said. "Who would want to be put in that position?"

The suit and ties laughed in agreement, one tilting his glass toward her in a salute. My mouth went as dry as crumbled plaster. I wanted to tell them, with the anger I felt, about all the respectable black businesspeople I knew, the folly of forfeiting the buying power of black America, and to ask how they could disrespect me to my face.

As I stewed, those people chattered on, the moment nothing to them. The official on my right had missed the whole thing, talking to people on his other side. I rose to my feet slowly and deliberately, my face flushed. A few seats away to my right, my boss caught my eye. He searched my face anxiously, and I knew he'd heard it. His lips were parted as he waited to see what I would do.

"Excuse me," I said, walking behind the laughing people's chairs and out of the restaurant into the gravel parking lot. My boss was right on my heels.

"I can't work like this," I said, the words scalding like boiling soup.

"No, wait," he said, and tried to explain. He said she didn't know I was black. I was so light she mistook me. His right hand splayed open in a pleading gesture. I studied the cleft in his chin, framed by lantern light on a white fence behind him. He said after the New York boss told him I was African American, he held a meeting last Friday to tell everyone in our office there would be a black manager, so they'd be ready. These managers from other departments probably hadn't been told, he said.

Don't leave, he kept saying. He'd see they were spoken to. The company's affirmative action policy would be enforced. It's just that I was the first black employee, let alone manager, in Baton Rouge. He saw it would take some doing to get it right. "I'm sorry." he said. "Please, come back in."

If I did, that meant plowing through their invisible rules of white supremacy just to do the work I was qualified and ready to do. Whites were the insiders, the ones with assumed acceptability, trustworthiness, and the right to be their unfiltered selves. So, who did that make me? The exhausted outsider doing my management assignments, yoked to a team of bigots?

"If you make it clear to them that this is unacceptable, I will go back in," I said.

The next morning, that woman called first thing. She said she wouldn't have said it if she had known I was black. I let her know how offended I was for myself and for black businesses. She was very sorry. I didn't believe her, but I had to accept the apology if I wanted to stay on that job. I thanked her for calling to say so, noting to myself that she as much as admitted she would have said that exact thing if I had been white.

A colleague named Donna, a put-together white woman about my age, invited us to dinner at her place. She had a lovely apartment on the second floor of a new complex in a convenient location. Over dessert, she offered the place to us. She was going to Alabama for six weeks and needed a house sitter. Would we like to stay in her apartment during that time while we found our own place?

Donna was a white southerner who not only trusted us African American newcomers with her things but also became a good friend. We were so grateful for the comforts of her apartment; the terms were worked out that evening.

Other whites were friendly, including neighbors in the building and several of my white thirtysomething office mates. I hung out with my management peers and one of them became a regular tennis partner of Luther's.

But it was hard for us Yankees to read the racial tea leaves in Baton Rouge. On the one hand were the white friends we made and the sugarcoated southern hospitality most people heaped on their greetings. On the other was the bald-faced prejudice other whites felt licensed to spew. We decided that dichotomy was the ambiguity that comes with any changing times and changing ways. So, we would not take on the jerks but would focus on our fit with the best of the South's progress. The proof that it had progressed was in our socializing with whites, something Daddy would never have dreamed of forty years ago back in Georgia.

On the hunt for a house to buy, I found new construction in a subdivision that buzzed with crews framing, painting, and unloading plumbing fixtures. There, a house was in our price range, with ideal size, amenities, and proximity to the interstate for commuting. The developer's on-site salesman eagerly promoted its features to me, pointing out the wide roof overhang that blunted the searing sun, the upgraded carpeting and tile, and the extra storage in the laundry room. He opened doors for me and pumped my interest by suggesting ways to include whatever I wanted. Back in his office, he said to bring my husband to see the place. His houses were selling fast.

"Y'all going to come today, after he gets off work?" he asked.

"Yes, when he gets home, we'll be back."

Luther and I skipped dinner to go straight to the house that had been left open for us. We bypassed the sales office in case he didn't like the property. That way, we wouldn't have to go through a hard sell with the agent.

I drove slowly through the newly made streets so Luther could look around. It seemed a mini town was under construction, with everything from several pristinely painted and landscaped new houses, to the cement slab foundations of others, with piles of lumber, roof shingles, and rolls of grassy sod on many plots.

We walked through the chosen house and admired the good-sized rooms, the kitchen's avocado self-cleaning oven, and the prospects of having a cement patio for outdoor living.

"I love how it's all new," Luther said. "Sparkling and state of the art. This boy from the projects is going to own a house with a lawn, backyard, and extra bedrooms." We decided to figure out an offer and go up to the office to talk with the agent right then. We sat on the floor in the sunny living room as Luther ran some numbers on his pocket calculator. We'd seen enough houses to know there wasn't much bargaining room in this hot market, so we decided on a strategy with a starting bid and a final bid.

We pulled up in the office driveway in the same car the salesman saw me in earlier. When I stepped out, he rubbed his hands together and smiled broadly. Then his eyes darted in alarm from me to my milk-chocolate husband getting out, then back to me.

"No, no, NO. Is that your husband?" he said, running backward into the office. He closed the door before we got there. Then we heard the lock catch. His eyes bugged out at us through the glass top half of the door. "I'm not selling to you," he called through the glass.

"We have the money, no problem," Luther called back.

"Naw, I cain't sell to no niggers. If I do, I cain't sell none of these other houses. Go on, now, git!" He yanked the shade down.

Luther's lips stuck out, pressed together like a platypus.

"That's illegal," I said. "He can't do that."

"Of course it's illegal. He invited you back because he thought you were white. Now get in the car, please." He wasn't waiting around to see what else might happen. Luther kept his eye on that office door until he pulled away. "Just forget it," he said.

"We could sue," I persisted.

"No, we're not going to do that. Let's find something else. I'm not getting into a battle with these white people down here. Clearly this isn't New York where you *might* win."

We sought out a white real estate agent to negotiate for us and bought an existing home in an established neighborhood without incident. Our neighbors were white, but right across the road was another development with all African American residents. They lived in tiny houses smaller than any I'd ever seen. Up the road was a fancier all-black development. Like where I grew up in the North, de facto segregation defined these neighborhoods. But unlike Buffalo's redlining that kept us out, Baton Rouge had entire black subdivisions where people intentionally chose to build or buy. Because they were barred in other ways, they stayed with their own to be spared the grief of dealing with white people in their home neighborhoods, a concept we transplants had failed to grasp.

11

A LINGERING SMOKY ODOR

When Luther got home from his new job, he went to see how the citrus plaid couch, delivered that day, looked with the Baton Rouge sunshine streaming through the window. Pleased, he slipped his arm around my waist. "You've made our house mighty nice, baby. It's beginning to feel like home."

Our consolation prize house was a three-bedroom ranch in an older neighborhood of small quarter-acre lots, the nicest we could comfortably afford. The day we closed, Luther had planted a palm tree in the backyard where we could see it from the dining room, a flag planting of our conversion to southerners.

After dinner, we snuggled up on our new couch, watching TV, me in my nightgown. About halfway through the program, an insistent banging started on the front door, so loud Luther and I both jumped. He approached the door cautiously while I ran back to the bedroom to pull a dress over my head. I heard the door latch open, then nothing.

"Come out here," Luther said.

He stood just inside the threshold, looking ahead like he was nailed in place. Standing beside him, I saw nobody was out there, anywhere. The street was silent and dark, except for the blaze illuminating the night sky. On our front lawn, flames jumped off a burning wooden cross, hammered into our lawn near a tree.

"Good God Almighty," I said, a sharp tingle electrifying my spine.

We took in that symbol of hate, scared to go out. Scanning our hundred-foot frontage and then the street, we couldn't see anybody moving. It was eerie, how still the night was, no neighbor coming outside when a fire crackled on a crucifix. Luther stepped out a few feet, and when no one appeared or spoke, he ran for the garden hose and tried to subdue the flames.

"Do you think they're going to kill us?" I whispered.

He hesitated. "Not tonight, I don't. There's no mob in sheets out here. Otherwise we'd already be hurt, or dead."

I called the police on the dining room wall phone, pulling the curly cord to the window to see if anybody was hiding out back.

"What's the nature of your emergency?" the responder asked.

"There's a cross burning on our lawn," I shouted.

"Anybody hurt?"

"No."

He took the address and said, "Do not go outside. We're on our way."

I lit up the property with all the outdoor lights and told Luther to let the hose go and come back in. Inside, he pulled me down to the floor and put his finger to his lips. Somebody might still be out there, he said. And there we crouched, listening and watching, pressing our fears into the wall we braced against.

Blue lights flashed as squad cars sped up to the house, stopping sharply at crazy angles in the street. Uniformed policemen waited beside their cars until the ranking officer stepped out, dressed in a wide-brimmed hat with a thick band around it, the kind a Canadian Mountie would wear. We turned on the dining room light and let him in the carport door. His men headed over to the cross.

"Y'all sit down here to the table," he said, without introduction, and began to interview us. What were we doing when the knock came on the door? Did we see anybody? Had we had arguments with anyone?

Who did we think did this? Where were we from? What were we doing in Baton Rouge? How long had we been in this house?

"Y'all stay there and don't come out," he said, walking toward the curb. In the blue lights, his all-white officers gathered around for instructions. Then, one guarded the front of our house while the others fanned out in the dark. One moved slowly through the backyard with a flashlight.

Luther shook his head, his lips pressed into a flat line. We waited at our table, the one where we ate our meals and admired the palm tree, the table where we got up extra early in the morning to play three games of Scrabble before work. "Best two out of three," Luther always said, "so we have an undisputed champion of the day."

I squeezed his hand as the minutes crawled by, my mind running wild with scenarios from Luther swinging from a tree to a court conviction that sent those bastards to prison. But with Luther's stern eyes doing the talking, I knew not to up the ante by saying those things out loud. So, we waited, steeped in our impotent fright.

The uniforms returned to talk with the chief, who stood wide-legged in the street, his arms crossed. I couldn't hear, so I tried to interpret what was going on by their gestures. One shook his head, another pointed down the street. A third hunched his shoulders like "I don't know." Their talk was too calm; nobody running around or shouting like they meant to catch somebody.

When the chief came inside, he motioned for us to sit down at the table while he stood over us. "Well," he said, "you must be some good nigras." Luther shot a hard look at me when I opened my mouth. With one small nod of his head left, he told me to keep quiet. His men had talked to our neighbors, the chief went on, and nobody had any complaints *about us*. It was impossible to process much of what he said after that, something about not finding any suspects.

"Call if you have more trouble," he said.

Luther raised his hand to shake, but the chief had already turned to go. When he was a few steps away, the click of Luther's tongue was as loud as a soda can popping.

I clutched a handful of his shirt and asked, "Are we safe?"

He led me to the couch and held me, rocking gently. "Shhh," he said, "shhh," then reached under the coffee table for the phone directory. "I'm calling the builder," Luther said. "He's the only one in this town we can trust."

It was true. We hardly knew anybody in Baton Rouge when that black contractor had invited us to Thanksgiving. A generation older than us, that six foot three manly man had sprinkled stories of the legion atrocities perpetrated against Baton Rouge blacks between showings of his too-expensive houses. He said we Yankees must be crazy, moving south to a place like Baton Rouge.

Luther's call the night of the cross burning woke the builder up. His tone went from foggy to furious when he understood what happened to us. Minutes later he parked his pickup in our driveway and strode through with a warlike gait and a piercing focus, a rifle gripped in his right hand. There was a power in him born of a burning rage.

Without saying hello, the builder started. "We been fighting these goddamned peckerwoods down here for years. But I got something right here for 'em." His belligerence was one with the big gun he set upright on its wooden butt right beside him at the table. He turned to me. "Get me something to drink, darlin', would you? Bourbon if you have it."

When I brought back the bottle and glasses, he poured a double and threw it back. Leaning in, he said he was going to take over our "situation." Luther pulled his chair closer.

"Now, listen," he said. "Y'all have to stop wearing your fear. It's in your eyes, your backs, your voices. They're like wild dogs," he said. "You show fear, they attack. Understand?"

He wanted us to know what happened to other black families who moved into white neighborhoods. They all got death threats. One got a handwritten note in their curbside mailbox when their kid brought in the mail. "MOVE OR DIE," it said. They left the house, sold at a loss, and went somewhere else. He didn't know where.

Another hadn't even unpacked when the phone calls started. The phone rang off the hook at all hours and whoever answered, man, woman, or child, was called a dead nigger. The wife and kids went to stay with her family. But the man stood on his front lawn and howled, "I am a man! I am a man!" The builder and other black men in town made a show of their guns on his property, which put a stop to the harassment. But that family moved away, too.

"The peckerwoods won back then," the builder said. "But we gonna put a stop to this."

"Were those men going to shoot somebody?" Luther asked.

"If they had to."

"What about the police?" Luther asked.

The builder snorted. "You mean the police okeydoke? Half of them are in the Klan, don't you know? They could've sent the people who set your fire."

He said since we were from up north, we didn't understand how it was. He saw how naive we were when we asked about building in white subdivisions, before he showed us the black ones. Did we even know we were smack dab in the middle of Klan country where David Duke, the Grand Wizard, held huge cross-burning rallies for the faithful in white robes and hoods?

"Don't expect to get justice in Louseyanna. Down here blacks only get Just-Us," he said. "Those same freedom fighters are still 'round here. They'll bring their guns tonight and camp out here 'til this bull crap stops. The white man will know we're not afraid of no crackers if we shoot one of 'em."

"What do you mean, shoot?" Luther asked, eying the big man.

The builder poured another shot. It would go like this. Some men would guard the house around the clock, in shifts. They would stay until they were sure no more white folks were coming back. If they had to, they'd shoot—to make it plain we would not be run off.

"Wait now," Luther said, shaking his head. "I'm not down with shooting folks."

"Might not have to shoot them cowards, once they see our threat and we make some noise. But if we have to, we will shoot."

He sat back in his chair, locking eyes with Luther. "OK?"

Luther stroked his moustache a few times. "Can't do it, man. It's too violent."

"Me neither," I said, shaking my head. A race war in my living room? I didn't know which was crazier, the white racists or the black freedom fighters.

Luther put his hand on the builder's shoulder. "Man, I'm grateful. But see, the only gun I ever held was when my pop drug me hunting one time. Just like I couldn't shoot the deer in front of us, I can't be part of shooting people."

"Then what you gonna do?"

"I don't know, but I'm gonna take my chances 'til I figure something out."

The builder grunted and stood silent for a moment. Then he poured us each a shot. "I'll be here if you change your mind," he said, and raised his glass. "No matter what, take care of this gal here."

Their handshake was a brothers' pact, one we knew would stand whenever needed. He moved down the driveway, peering closely around our property. He rustled the monkey grass border curled over its own long blades like cotton pickers, poking with the barrel of his rifle like a western lawman.

I looked over to see what the cross looked like up close, but it was gone. The police had taken it. Instead, I saw they'd pulled us back into their time warp, tried to negate all we'd worked for, and left us with only a lingering smoky odor, the hole in our lawn, and their slap in our face.

The next day Luther and I went to see Larry, a more mild-mannered black man than the builder, to tell him about the cross burning. He gave us his advice in his family room, where his collection of long guns and handguns were locked inside a glass wall display that centered the room.

"You gotta defend yourself against these rednecks," Larry said. "Most everybody down here carries something. You should too."

We didn't say so, but of course we had no intention of getting a gun. Nobody in New York we knew carried a gun, or thought one was necessary. As far as I knew, guns were for criminals, hunters, and crazies. Not for people like us.

Our black friends from Luther's job asked if we weren't going to move. Their concern palpable, one asked, "Is staying in that house worth it?"

In the next days, our house was egged, then another morning we found garbage strewn on the lawn: coffee grounds and dirty diapers, empty soup cans and newspapers, leftover chili and chicken bones. Luther called the police, who said they couldn't do anything about it after the fact. So, we cleaned it up and hosed down the house and grass.

We were just sick, sitting on that citrus couch. The barrage of racism in housing, schools, jobs, and just common decency we'd endured earlier in our lives now looked like mere waystations on the road to hate this big. But as weary as that made us, we were angry and insulted too. Enough so that it was plain we had to straighten our backs and not let these white people take us down.

12

TOO THROUGH

L uther woke up that Sunday morning, his knees and ankles so stiff he couldn't move them. His face had erupted overnight into a raw rash, his skin flaking like scales off a fish. When I tried to move his legs toward the edge of the bed, he moaned. "Stop. You're killing me."

Tylenol and the heating pad didn't help, so the doctor said to meet him at the hospital. Luther got into his loosest clothes and house slippers, us both straining in the already ridiculous heat. He hobbled to the car, leaning on me as I held him up by the back of his pants. We didn't shower, but once in the car I regretted it as the smell of my ripe sweat filled the space.

The doctor examined Luther, signed admission papers, and ordered tests before leaving. Luther lay on a gurney in a dingy hall, waiting for his room. After a long while, I had to squat to rest my legs. When way too much time had passed, I went to the desk.

"Excuse me," I said, "Luther Johnson hasn't been transferred to his room yet. Do you know what we're waiting for?"

The attendant didn't look up from her papers. But she did sniff loudly. "There's no room for a black man now," she said flatly. As if it was obvious that Luther should continue to lay there without treatment just so a white man didn't have to be in the same room with him. Humiliated and angry, I chose to bite my Yankee tongue and feign submissiveness like other blacks waiting in the emergency room. Arguing with her could sabotage his care further.

Once in his room, Luther fell asleep, moaning when he tried to move. He stayed like that as the days dragged by in a medical mire of misdiagnoses, from malaria to a spinal disorder, and back to a barrage of tests that turned up nothing. Then one morning Luther lay catatonic, suspended in a coma-like state, with only his steady breath to show he was alive. And there he lay in that netherland without me, for so many more days than I can now measure.

My only respite from the hell my life had become was clearing the weeds from our front flower beds. In that humid heat, they grew thick and deep, yielding only when I avenged my demons on them. On a late afternoon while wrangling a batch out, I hardly registered a motorcycle's vrooming up the street. Suddenly something exploded in my face, it's singeing heat too near my eyes. Clusters of firecrackers pop-pop-popped with their smoke plumes rising, long after the per-petrator rode away.

I ran inside and closed the drapes, thinking they could have blinded me. I lay on my bed crying, afraid and exhausted from the constant dread of what else might happen. Depression overtook me as I unbut-toned my shorts to loosen the waistband that cut deep welts into my middle. I'd probably gained thirty pounds since the trouble started, looking for comfort in bakeries and fried chicken joints. But just as eating hadn't saved me, Luther couldn't save me, the police wouldn't save me, and I wouldn't let the builder save me. I drifted into a fitful sleep, not knowing what would save me.

―――――――――

Luther was awake the next morning, frantically straining against gauze restraints that tied his wrists and ankles to the bed. He begged me, inco-herently, to get him loose while the staff insisted the restraints kept him from getting hurt. The doctor came in with no explanation for Luther's swollen joints, rash, catatonia, misdiagnoses, or state of mind. What he recommended was best for my husband was to transfer him upstate to the Louisiana State psychiatric hospital. He handed me the already prepared committal papers to sign, apparently expecting compliance. Luther wasn't mentally ill, he was sick. Yet this white man was ready to leave him indefinitely in some waste pile of Negro neglect and probable abuse. I said we needed a cure, not a warehouse, and would look for other options. At the hallway payphone, I called the builder for an opinion.

"Naw, no ma'am," he said. "Don't even think about signing that mess. Black people who go in there never come out."

I called Luther's pop in Harlem.

"Sounds like that there lupus he had back in his twenties," Pop said, "when he was so sick for all those months. Physical and mental."

How could that be? When we'd gotten engaged, Luther told me he'd had a blood disease called lupus, but that it was behind him. So I never investigated lupus before we stood under the flowered arch in my family church and said our vows. Now Pop gave me the number of the New York lupus specialist who had treated Luther a decade before.

That doctor told me lupus was never "behind" you. It is an incurable disease often found in blacks that destroys vital organs and can be fatal. Pop got on the next flight to Baton Rouge, then escorted Luther on the transfer up to New York to be treated by that specialist.

I had to stay behind in that house by myself to keep my job's medical insurance, the only one we had. A frightening pile of medical bills on the dining table had already reached well into six figures, and now there was just my one salary coming in instead of two. I could afford to visit Luther in New York only one weekend a month. In those few days I'd see Luther, discuss his case with doctors, and try to figure out a future with his family's support.

Back at work in Baton Rouge, I did my best to keep managing a team that sold new technology to local businesses. That focus was the one sane part of my day. We strategized on prospective sales, and I took turns accompanying each of my team members on calls, assessing opportunities and debriefing afterward. When it was the big fifty-something man's turn, the one whose resentment for my black young female Yankee self was obvious, he glared over his glasses and said, "I don't need you to go."

Because I was twenty-six and stupidly wanted to assert my authority, I said we *would* go. He drove us in the company car out of town to a small business with a basic system we could upgrade. Once there, he and the older white owner did a lot of back slapping and coffee drinking but negligible business. Back in the car, I explained what products he could have proposed and what he might have done differently. Red faced, he refused to engage.

He started the engine and drove down a sparsely populated road for ten minutes, ignoring me. Bulging blood vessels pulsed in his neck before he turned for what I expected to be the next customer call. Instead it was a small dirt road bordered by tall tangled weeds that dead-ended out of sight. He killed the engine and turned to me, his eyes boring into mine. And I saw it in him, the bone-deep hate that could kill me. Like Chaney, Goodman, and Schwerner whom the Klan buried in a dam wall in Mississippi, nobody would be able to find me. With my thighs frying on the scorching upholstery, I forced myself to glare back, even as I prayed to be forgiven my sins.

I don't know how long we tried to stare down each other's souls on that day in the Louisiana backwoods where my father warned me not to go. I tried to break his threat by turning away and looking out the front window. The pull of his eyes burned into my cheeks, but I would not look back. Alert to any move that big man might make, my every muscle was ready to jump out. We sat there, silent and seething, before he finally turned the engine on and headed back to the city.

On the way, we drove past the state capitol, where all too fittingly a Confederate flag flew prominently. Its message was the same as the salesman's: white people could get away with hurting blacks in Louisiana. Maybe that salesman had been the one who already tried, burning that cross on our lawn.

That night, several helmeted men raced up on my front lawn on roaring motorcycles. They leaned side to side until the smooth carpet of our mowed and edged grass was ripped up. I called the police to come right then, to catch them in the act.

"We can't make it over there," the officer said. "There's a football game at LSU. Every thang in town and ever'body is tied up."

I walked in circles in the living room, peeping out from behind the drapes at the vandals nobody would stop. They must have known I was alone in the house. Luther's car hadn't moved from the carport the whole time he was hospitalized. What was I going to do when the evildoers came back? Next time they might do their worst. Beat me. Rape me. Kill me. I could call Mama and Daddy again, fifteen-hundred miles away up in Buffalo, and give them another sanitized version of what was going on. All Daddy would say is to run, like he and Grandma did when they *escaped* from Georgia in the 1930s. But I had to stay to keep our medical insurance, so why tell them anything?

With nobody to help me, I had to do something to take care of myself. I had Larry take me shopping for a gun.

The one-story building stood alone on a nearly deserted street with a large GUNS sign across the front. Inside, we were the only customers. A hefty white clerk smiled; the glasses set on top of his head glinting in the very bright lights. Larry said we needed some protection for the lady.

"Why sure," the clerk said, sweeping his arm across a mind-boggling array of weaponry. Behind him, long rifles and shotguns were mounted on the wall in rows. Farther down were more elaborate automatics that I associated with soldiers and criminals. And in front of me were locked glass display cases, the type you'd find in a jewelry store. There, black handguns lay on their sides, with barrel lengths ranging from snub nosed to arm's length. Their handles were black, with a few fancier ones in brown wood or what looked like mother-of-pearl. Was I supposed to pick one I liked, like a piece of jewelry?

"Let's see a lady's handgun," Larry said. "It's her first."

The clerk put a few guns on top of the case. "Ma'am, let's find you one that fits your hand so you can handle it. See, the right fit gives less recoil and a more enjoyable shoot."

Enjoyable? Here I was scared to death I'd have to shoot somebody to keep from getting shot myself, and he thought this was fun? We found a couple I could wrap my hand around easily. Larry steered me to those with long barrels because the longer the bullet rode in the barrel, the more accurate hit I'd make.

"But those are not so good for a concealed carry," the salesmen offered, "'less you got a big handbag or a holster."

I saw how to pull back the hammer, then press the trigger fast with the same hand. In fifteen minutes, I had a right-sized six-shooter I could aim at a spot on the wall and use to blow a Baton Rouge bigot to kingdom come.

I learned to use my gun in an open country field set up for target practice. Out there, I bumbled through the first steps—getting the feel of the unloaded weapon, picking it up and pointing in one fast move, until I got comfortable. Next, I aimed at empty beer and soda cans set on a chopped-off tree stump. When I first used ammunition, my bullets went wide, into the woods and the ground. But one sunlit evening out in that field, I planted my feet, held still, and let the bullet clear the barrel for a straight shot and sent those cans jumping. When I had enough skill to hit a good spot on the circular target mounted on a tripod, I was miserable. I could make anybody sorry who attacked me, with a gun I wanted no part of.

The revolver stayed on my nightstand. It was fully loaded and cocked, with the handle positioned for a fast grab. And there it stayed until the night a noise in the kitchen woke me up. I sat up in bed and listened. Was that something creaking? Somebody was inside the house, moving toward the bedrooms. I pushed the covers back and put my bare feet on the floor. I was not about to let them kill me in my own bed. Adrenaline poured through me as I reached for the gun. It felt good in my hand as I threaded my finger onto the trigger. At the bedroom doorway, I stopped to listen.

CLACK. Somebody had cocked *their* trigger.

I inched down the dark hallway toward the living room, squinting in every corner since I'd forgotten to put on my glasses. Pretty sure nobody was in the living room, I set my feet wide apart to steady me, and lifted the revolver to my good eye. Aiming through the dining room and into the open kitchen behind it, I stroked the trigger with my finger, searching for the intruder.

CLACK.

Suddenly, I recognized the clack was my refrigerator's thermostat adjusting. There was nobody in my house after all. They weren't coming after all this time. Luther had been right the night the cross was burned. If they wanted to kill us, we'd have already been dead.

I wiped sweat off my brow with the loaded gun still in my hand. In that moment, I saw myself—a crazed black person ready to shoot a white man in a state where I could never be acquitted.

I fixed a two-finger Jack and ginger with plenty of ice and sat in the dark on Luther's living room recliner. When I calmed down, another time somebody's pride in homeownership was trampled on came to mind . . . my parents, when they bought their first and only house in 1958.

———————

I was ten then. As the pile of cardboard boxes in the living room grew higher, Mama hummed on. "Que Sera, Sera" came from the back hall by the coal bin.

We were moving from our backlot apartment with its potbelly stove and the amped voices of choirs and preachers at the church next door. Daddy and Mama had saved for fifteen years so we could move into our own house across town, in the beautiful Cold Spring neighborhood. There we would own, not rent, and live in it all by ourselves.

That place on Florida Street cost my parents $8,000, financed with a thirty-year mortgage and monthly payments of $89. An NAACP man from church had talked to Daddy about moving to Cold Spring. He said not to worry about moving out there because when his family had integrated that part of Buffalo, they had no trouble at all buying, or when they moved in. In fact, our house on Florida Street was surrounded by white families like the Siegrists and Gagliones, neighbors on either side of us.

The night we moved in, Daddy poured champagne from the gift bottle the sellers left, even giving a little to each of us three kids.

"Here's to our American dream come true," he said, raising his cup.

I didn't like the sour wine that fizzed all over my nose but understood what a big deal that house was. My parents clicked pink plastic cups and linked arms to drink. When they kissed, Daddy's eyes were wet as he smiled down at Mama. He had more pride in his eyes at that moment than any other time I can remember. And I was as proud of him as I can ever remember being—the black man at the head of our family, the breadwinner who got us a house, the father who loved my mama.

What Mama loved most about the new neighborhood was Humboldt Parkway. That green space, just two blocks from the house, was where she would stroll among the sprawling canopies of maples and elms planted in lines down the mall. Humboldt joined a string of other public landscaped parks meandering through Buffalo, forming another of Olmstead's curated Emerald Necklaces through American cities. We had been to those green spaces many times, when Mama had driven miles to enjoy them when we were younger.

"Some people want to live by the lake," Mama said. "But the parkway is my oasis, with its grass and trees, where we can breathe." Once the house was set up, we started walking over there. The boys ran free while the two of us, neither with an athletic bone in our bodies, walked in the fresh air of the grounds.

Unbeknownst to us, the realtors were blockbusting. They scared white owners who feared losing value by living near Negroes into selling while selling those houses to more blacks. The white exodus flipped our predominantly white neighborhood to black within a couple years after we moved in. Realtors got paid plenty, sacrificing our black dreams to earn commissions on sales to us, as well as from the new suburban homes purchased by the fleeing whites. If I'd internalized that lesson and not been so sure access to housing in white neighborhoods was open to me in Baton Rouge, that cocked gun wouldn't have been in my lap right then.

My parents watched the evening news one night, noting a traffic jam with streams of red taillights barely inching along. Some official said the traffic on local roads had built to untenable messes every morning and night from the new suburban commuters trying to get back and forth to downtown jobs. The congestion had to be relieved, and the solution was to build a new expressway.

Daddy sat on the living room couch, talking back to the TV. "Those white commuters just left Cold Spring and moved to those suburbs. That's why. Report that."

"There's no place to put a highway," Mama said. "All the land between the suburbs and downtown is residential. It's talk, that's all."

"No, babe," Daddy said. "Those politicians downtown will put it right through Cold Spring." He said downtown didn't care about us. Our neighborhood had become a pain in the ass for the white people who had to waste time crossing it on the way to work.

"Since none of them live here anymore," he said, "we'll be targeted for that road. Watch and see."

The expressway route ran straight down Humboldt Parkway.

When construction started, twelve-year-old David and I walked up to Humboldt to see what was going on, even though we'd been told not to because it was too dangerous. We heard the deafening boom from bulldozers driven straight into those statuesque elms before we got there. We saw a tree pushed up and out of the serene grove, its enormous root system thundering onto the dirt.

Boom! Another tree thudded to the ground. Boom! Then another and another toppled over. An army of men in safety glasses with power tools sawed off branches from felled trees. The high-pitched squeal of woodchippers ground the smaller limbs into sawdust as bulky trucks grunted into a start and hauled away the trunks.

"What are they doing?" I yelled over the noise.

"Destroying it, just like Daddy said they would."

"They can't do that!"

"Wake up, my sister," David said. "White people never run out of ways to mess us up."

Weeks later I went back to see what the project looked like. Thick mud caked over my shoes and socks up in front of St. Francis de Sales church. Men in hard hats operated a battlefield of earthmovers, digging deep underneath where the parkway had been, hauling away dirt and boulders in loud, chugging trucks spewing black soot. Down at the corner of Delavan Avenue, the hole they were making seemed big enough to drop in the entire Peace Bridge from Buffalo over the Niagara River to Canada.

A fork was taking shape in the road. One branch turned right about where Humboldt ended and the other swung a little left. The design saved all of Delaware Park, the next link in the Emerald Necklace, over in the neighborhood where white people lived. But on our black side there was that mammoth hole and dirt floating thickly in the air, covering the houses and church. And making me feel filthy.

I reached down and plucked a wood chip the size of an apple wedge from the dirt and put it my pocket, a souvenir of how helpless we were to stop the destruction. It sat on the little wooden desk Daddy had made for my room, a daily reminder of ruination.

When the work was done, Daddy drove us on the new expressway. Giant walls banked the sunken road, holding back the gutted earth behind them, topped with ugly chain-link fencing. Litter had already collected at their bottoms. Not one living green thing remained. Not anywhere. And the city had divided us from friends on the other side. Only three cross streets were left above, meaning we had to walk many blocks out of the way to get over there.

"Our community was raped," Daddy said, driving on. "You see, it's every bit as prejudiced up here in the North as it is down South. They're just slicker about it. You don't realize they're going to dig your grave 'til the mayor signs off on the shovels."

"But we have our own home and garden," Mama said. "They can't take that away from us. We're going to be happy with what we do have." She kept on making flower beds in the backyard from bushes and bulbs and bags of manure, working in bone meal and ground eggshells to feed them. Mama would have her green space, even if it was small. She got on her knees in that dirt for the next thirty years, wearing the girdle she would not be seen without, planting roses and peonies, snap dragons, poppies, and gladiolas outside our back door. The luscious fragrance from her purple lilac bushes was so powerful I could smell them coming up the driveway.

My drink finished, I got up from my Baton Rouge recliner and went into the bedroom closet to fish out a shoebox of old souvenirs. Pushing aside ticket stubs and expired student ID cards, I felt the rough edges of that wood chip from Humboldt Parkway at the bottom. I pulled it out and rolled it around the palms of my hands.

No way would Luther and I stay in our first house the way my parents did theirs. No, I was through—too through with black life in the South. We had to get out of Baton Rouge. I laid the wood chip beside the cocked revolver on the nightstand and kept it there. It symbolized my mission, to make a new life for us while Luther got well.

Of the several jobs on the East Coast I'd applied for, a great marketing position in New Jersey was offered. We'd be an hour from Luther's family and the lupus specialist in New York, whose continual care was essential. "Mr. Johnson," he'd said, "if only you had come to us sooner, we could have prevented some of the irreversible damage done to your vital organs."

We sold the Baton Rouge house and moved to a bigger one in a tiny central Jersey town in 1978. Luther came home after ten months in the hospital and landed the government engineering job he held for the rest of his short life.

As we got in bed one night, he said, "C'mon, baby. Give me that wing and spoon me." For the first time in a year we lay there happily snuggling as a soft breeze floated through the sheers at our bedroom window.

It had taken that long for us to reconcile to America's truth, that racism is embedded in the country's fabric, down in the marrow of the malicious, the unaware, and the disinterested. It was true in Louisiana or New York, that despite the changed national narrative and law, white people, including the neighborhood children chanting "Nigger, nigger, nigger," behind our new hedges, could not be trusted to do right by us.

At least, we hoped New Jersey was a better chance to live safely.

13

JUST LISTEN

I picked apart that surreal hour with my white people at the airport a million times. No longer able to focus on those endless slides presented in conference rooms or where I left my basket in the supermarket aisles, that fleeting connection to my mother's sister haunted me.

Because Dorothy turned off her cooking and rushed to come meet me that day. Because she seemed thoughtful about Mama running away, apparently weighing the reasons she did so. Because she hadn't shown outrage or rejection or any of the devastating reactions Mama feared. The truth was out. Well, all but Mama not being dead, and the Boehles were decent about it.

I needed another chance to really talk with them about what it meant to be related. Yet Mama was so traumatized that they knew about me, she wouldn't agree to any more contact.

"What about me?" I complained to Luther as we wandered through a hardware store. How was I going to understand my white blood, the reason I went looking for Mama's family in the first place? That one measly cup of coffee with Dorothy wasn't enough to understand squat.

He asked me what else I wanted to know.

"Well, for one thing, do the Boehles mean anything to my identity?" Understanding their lives and family tree would give me a truer sense of myself, like when old Aunt Willie laid out Daddy's black family photos. Would I be able understand those relatives from an all-white world? Was their kind of white different from Mama's sort-of white, bred in her ghetto life? Did any part of them fit in my soul? "I don't understand what having a white family means," I said. "But I have to."

"I see you're not going to quit," Luther said. "You're talking about spending time with the Boehles, having a lot of frank conversation with them. Just how you gonna pull that off?" He wandered away to the screw bins, scrutinizing each in his engineer's paradise.

"First you were on fire to go find them," he said in the car. "Just to look at them, to prove they existed. You dropped out of the sky and rewrote Dorothy's life for her. She gave you the civilized conversation you wanted. But now you want more."

The meeting with Dorothy had been all about Mama's disappearing. So, I didn't find out who the Boehles really were. For me. I didn't even know if they were prejudiced, or if Dorothy would acknowledge me as a niece. Or if I wanted to acknowledge them. That's what would make them a real part of me. Not just some random bloodline like my black grandma's raping white father somewhere in Lee County plantation Georgia.

I was sure Mama wanted to know more too; she just didn't think she could handle it. Just the night before she asked if any of Dorothy's girls in that picture looked like her. There had to be a way to move forward—hopefully with her, but without if she couldn't be convinced.

I buckled up for my work commute over two interstates. Out on that racetrack, I moved between cars from Pennsylvania going seventy miles per hour, bumper-to-bumper in a beat-the-clock melee through New Jersey to New York. Gray overcast skies matched my mood as I obsessed about getting Mama to be in touch with Aunt Dorothy.

Squeezing into the leftmost passing lane of four, I hugged the bumper in front of me. I became one with that unforgiving high-speed lane next to the cement barricade separating eastbound from westbound traffic.

Without warning, my steering wheel pulled sharply to the right where other speeding cars rode beside me. The car spun around, jerking my neck, to face oncoming traffic. I took my foot off the gas, gritted my teeth, and strained to reverse the wheel and get the car turned back, facing east again. The wheel moved on its own, frozen out of place. It pulled my shoulder so hard I thought it would come out of the socket. With no possibility of control, I had to let go.

"Oh God," I said, stomping on the useless, locked brakes. The car skidded on its own across the four-lane racetrack toward the other shoulder. A blur of cars swerved past me on both sides, in the din of their blaring horns.

As the certain collision barreled toward me, I locked eyes with the driver of an eighteen-wheeler facing me head-on. He was close enough, up in his cab, that I could see his green plaid shirt and dark moustache. The vision of all that weight and power slamming into my little Toyota made me close my eyes and give in to fate.

The car jerked sharply again, whiplashing my head as it skidded back across the highway toward the passing lane. But on that return slide the momentum slowed, and the car petered to a stop in the second lane. My eyes flew open to meet the trucker's, which were still locked on mine.

I sat still, trying to grasp what happened. Cars were scattered all over New Jersey I-80 eastbound. They faced New York, and I faced Pennsylvania. The racetrack was at a standstill, cars stopped as far as I could see. The lanes behind me were empty. In the height of rush hour, those cars had driven on, out of danger.

I scanned the highway slowly for crashes. An eerie confusion enveloped me when I realized all the cars were intact. I took off my seatbelt and gingerly examined my limbs while the whole interstate idled in wait. My arms and legs worked. There was no blood on me or the floor.

Shakily opening my door, I pushed myself out onto a still, quiet highway, leaned on the car, and tried to get my wits about me.

The truck driver climbed down and came to me. "You all right?"

"I think so."

"Black ice," he said. "You hit a patch of black ice. You can't hardly see it, but this time of year you got to watch for it, little lady." He pointed to some on the highway, nodded knowingly, and walked back to his truck. Cars toot-tooted their horns in celebration that our lives would go on.

The car started up OK. I made a U-turn to face New York and got off the highway at the next exit. Too shaken to drive farther, I went back home. At the house, I dropped my briefcase and purse at the door, went straight to the bedroom, and got in bed with my suit on. I called in sick and scooted down under the electric blanket.

I was lucky to be alive. Escaping that truck slamming into me was proof that tomorrow is not promised. So there, in the safety of my bed, I made up my mind: I was going to talk to my secret white family again, with or without Mama's permission.

That Saturday morning, I called David to enlist him in my plan. He was the sibling who held sway with my parents. He'd earned it, stopping by often, bringing them things, and taking them out. As the popular chairman of Buffalo's Juneteenth Freedom Festival, he made sure folks in the 'hood respected and helped our parents. During the blizzard of '78, he took his National Guard unit to dig out my parents, along with the priority municipal sites they'd been assigned to.

"What's happening, Jody," he boomed in his always too loud voice. He called me by my little sister horse-tending stooge name from the cowboys and Indians games he and Charles Nathan starred in when we were kids. I always got run out of Dodge or arrested while they rode into the sunset.

I asked him how he thought Mama was handling the Dorothy news.

It meant a lot to her, he said. She talked about it all the time. And even though he wasn't much for finding the white people at first, he had to admit Mama was excited to hear about Dorothy and her kids.

"She could be even more excited," I said.

"How?"

"Since the Boehles didn't act the fool like you predicted, and they gave me their address, maybe if I told them Mama was still alive, they might take her back."

"You out of your mind, Sapphire?" he asked, putting me in my black place, as he loved to do.

"I want you to help me convince Mama it's worth a try."

"Tell you what I'm going do," he said. "I'm going send Roto-Rooter right over to snake out your Harvard brain. Didn't you have box seats when Mama said she didn't want any more to do with this?"

"Can't you just get her to consider it? So I won't be out here all by myself, trying to find out about the Boehles? They're your relatives too."

"Naw, little sis, I'm out. This is your thing and yours alone."

After fixing my coffee, I turned right around and called Mama to discuss my new proposition. Since she made me lie to her lost sister when I found her, Mama had stonewalled every idea I had to undo the lie. But I needed to tell Dorothy that Mama hadn't been dead all these years. So I could find out the truth about the white people whose blood ran in my own veins.

"No," leaked out of her. "Not again."

I explained she could just listen on the phone while I talked to Dorothy on a three-way call. Dorothy would be in Indianapolis, Mama in Buffalo, and me in New Jersey.

"You can do that?" she asked, unable to keep up with even the smallest technology changes.

I'd place the call from my office. Mama would stay completely quiet but could hear everything Dorothy had to say. I'd tell her sister the truth, that Mama was alive. Then Mama could judge for herself where Dorothy's heart was. After we hung up, then Mama could decide what to do.

"Why do you keep this up?" Mama asked. "When she finds out I'm living, she won't want me. It's been thirty-five years since I disappeared."

I told her if Dorothy was happy she was still alive, maybe they could get back together. If she wasn't, we'd hang up and forget about her. My own questions about my missing white people and what they had to do with my mixed identity would be written off and forever irrelevant. But was Mama's fear enough reason to miss this chance to see if she could get her family back? It didn't make sense to me, not for a woman with the guts to have run off with a black man to avoid lynching or prison in 1942.

Daddy was the one to persuade her. When they called back, for once he did the talking. He had told Mama he knew leaving her family hurt her deep down, even though she never said so. But he was the reason she left them. And he carried that burden all these years too. She had vowed not to ever look back, and she hadn't. At least not out loud. But he could see it. Like when Mama planned to name me Dorothy had I been born on her sister's birthday.

"I told your mother straight up," Daddy said, "I'd be relieved if marrying me didn't mean she was cut off from her sister her whole life. That's what changed her mind."

All my thirty-odd years I'd been mad about Daddy's drinking. But after facing my own life-altering bigots as an adult, I knew his Four Roses was his only escape from the racist injustices, disrespect, and fears he raged about as soon as he came through our door every night. And here he'd also carried this deep regret for his wife having to give up her people. I loved him then for convincing Mama to hear what Dorothy had to say. How could I not get over his drinking when he was the father who bore all those black burdens on our behalf the only way he knew how?

We went over the plan. I would do all the talking and Mama would remain silent. There would be with no coughing, no striking matches for Camels, no radio or TV in the background. Daddy would listen on the extension, then we would compare notes after we hung up with Dorothy.

On a day my boss was on a business trip, I locked my office door and asked the secretary not to disturb me. I stared at the phone sitting on my credenza. Would Dorothy be angry or reject Mama? Was I on crack? I took a deep breath and called Mama, then added Dorothy.

"Hi, Dorothy. It's Dolores." I intentionally left off *Aunt* until she had earned it. We went through pleasantries before I told her my purpose. "I hope to straighten out something I told you when we met. Because, well, I must apologize. I told you a lie."

"You lied to me?" She was incredulous, maybe accusing. "What lie? We aren't related?"

My back began to seize up with those cold stings, like hail pounding bare skin. The accompanying panic stressed me out, even as I pretended it didn't.

"Oh, we're related all right. But the lie was about my mother. See, she's still living. But she's scared to death to face you."

"She's alive? You say Ella is still living? Is that right?"

"Yes, she is living. That is right."

"Why would you lie about a thing like that?"

"I'm sorry, but before I came to Indiana my mother made me promise to say she was dead." I braced for her rebuke.

"But why? What possible reason could she have to say that?"

"She thinks you will hate her for running away so long ago without a word. But after the things you said to me, I thought you might feel otherwise. That you don't hate her."

"Hate my only sister? No! I could never hate my sister. If Ella is alive, I want to see her. I love her. Please, tell her there isn't anything to be afraid of."

A pitiful, thick wail drowned Dorothy out.

"That's your sister crying," I said. "I'm sorry, Dorothy, for not telling you she is on the line. Mama was supposed to only listen."

"What did you say?"

"You two are here on the same phone line together right now. Maybe one of you wants to say something to the other?"

"Ella, is it really you?" Dorothy said. "I love you, Ella. I've missed you so much. Don't be afraid. Oh, please, say something."

Through her sobs, Mama stuttered, "Yes, Dot . . . it's me . . . I love you too."

Dorothy cried as hard as Mama. Then suddenly I was crying too, about the thirty-six years of tears heaving up out of *them*. Dorothy said again she loved Mama. She forgave Mama. Forget about the past. She had an inconceivable, saintly kind of compassion and love, a kind I never knew existed. One I couldn't have given if I were in Dorothy's shoes.

For a few minutes we had a three-way breakdown. Sure, Mama and her sister were crying, but my executive facade crumbled too. The tough ghetto girl turned corporate badass bawled with them. I slumped in my ergonomic chair, wiping my tears on my good silk blouse.

"I want to see you, Ella, as soon as possible," Dorothy said. "We have to."

"I don't know," Mama said, barely able to speak, "after what I did."

"Forget about all that, Ella," Dorothy said. "Either I'll come to you or you come back home. Either way you want."

Mama said she needed time to think about that. Hearing Dorothy's voice was such a shock, she couldn't think straight. Mama didn't know if she could get past her guilt enough to face Dorothy. "Give me a chance, please, to get it in my head that you could still love me."

"I do love you," Dorothy said. "And I'll be waiting for you when you're ready."

———

Now that the door to my white family was open, I needed to figure out how to best explore my identity and talk about it with them. Over dinner with Luther, I asked his advice.

"You will have to open your heart," he said. "You've got some work to do." He asked if I could get past that cross burning and the suspicion that white folks don't mean us any good. They deserved a fair chance on their own merits. "If you can't, you will never know any more about your identity than you do today."

But what about keeping my guard up, I argued, to protect against any trouble? Did he mean to just open up to these unknown Boehles, who lived in the conservative heartland my parents had to flee in fear for their lives? If black people didn't like my white part, would these white people accept my black part?

Luther scraped the dishes slowly. "Just see if you find a sense of family between you, in your heart."

———

A few days later, Mama came around. She wanted to see her sister. But she was worried Dot's husband and kids might not feel kindly toward her. I promised to be with her during the visit, to make sure it went OK.

"She sure can't come to Buffalo," Mama said. Dorothy probably hadn't been around any Negroes, so visiting Mama's ghetto neighborhood might make her too scared. Mama didn't want the kind of problems her Clique Club friend Angela had when her sister Connie visited.

"Her sister came to Buffalo?" I asked. I thought her racist white family in Ohio didn't know about her black family in Buffalo.

Angela had confided to her closest sister that she had a black husband and three children in Buffalo. She begged Connie to come meet them and spend time all together, just once. When Connie finally agreed, she made some pretext to her own family and set out driving from Smalltown, Ohio.

Connie pulled up in front of the two-family house where Angela rented a flat, but she didn't get out. Angela and her black daughter, Sandra, dressed in their Sunday best, ran outside to greet her. Angela called to her excitedly to come on, but Connie didn't move. Instead she rolled her window down and motioned frantically for Angela to come around to the driver's side. Angela later said she had the clothes and hairdo of a princess, and the eyes of a crazy woman.

Connie was scared out of her mind around all the Negroes she saw. "They're all over your neighborhood," she said frantically. "Something bad is going to happen."

"But, but . . ." Angela started. Connie made a U-turn and sped off, straight back to Smalltown, without even waving good-bye.

Who were these white people, I wondered, and what was their problem? Could Dorothy pull a stunt like that? David thought anything was possible but wanted Mama to invite Dorothy to the 'hood, to prove she accepted black folks. Daddy thought Dot coming to stay in the ghetto was too much stress for everybody. Instead, Mama should go visit Dorothy back in her hometown. But Daddy said flatly he wasn't going.

"My being a black man will complicate the situation. They may not accept me, but that's not the point. The point is for your mother to get straight with her sister, and I don't want to spoil that. Maybe later, if the coast is clear. But I'm not going this first time."

We decided I would go to Indy with Mama, to help her, yes, but just as much, I reminded my family, because I wanted to get to know the Boehles for my own reasons. We had another three-way phone call with Dorothy to make arrangements.

When Mama and I boarded the plane in Buffalo, I smelled her Jean Nate, something she wore on special occasions. As soon as she settled into her seatbelt, her rosary beads clicked against each other. She told me twice the prayers would protect us. I told her twice I would, too. Midflight, tears started rolling down her face.

"Nothing's ever been harder than this," she said. She blew her nose so loudly and often that people across the aisle leaned in to see what was going on.

I gently told her to pull herself together. "This is the day you get your life back. It's the day you will also give me the missing part of mine. C'mon, be strong."

She nodded, and I ordered us each a ginger ale and one Jack Daniels mini. Mama drank her glass of soda with a splash of liquor without protest, even though she didn't drink. Then she handed me a box of Tic Tacs. "We can't smell like drunks when we meet Dorothy," she said.

When the plane landed, Mama waited until everybody else was off. After everyone deplaned, she still hadn't gotten up. The stewardess came back to our seats to help get us going.

"We're coming," Mama said, moving at a turtle's pace across the row. She stood in the aisle with her sixty-nine-year-old stooped shoulders, shrunken six inches from osteoporosis. She pulled herself up to her full height, now the size of a twelve-year-old boy. Mama tugged on the new wig that hid her thin hair to center it and checked that her good white enamel necklace was on straight.

Mama went down the aisle with steady determination, looked straight ahead, then stepped into the jetway.

14

THE VISIT

With her chin lifted and my arm through hers, Mama stopped at the exit to the gate. "You can let go now. I'm going out on my own. But please stay right behind me."

Glancing over her four-foot-eight frame as we stepped into the building, I spotted Dorothy watching our door. Most people had already left the area, so she was nearly alone. Mama had asked that nobody else come to the airport except Dorothy and her husband, so she wouldn't be overwhelmed.

Dorothy was dressed in just-plain-folks' polyester slacks and a wide cut overblouse. I couldn't tell if it was her intense eyes or her girth that made her seem so much taller than her five feet, one inch. Maybe my nerves were making her bigger.

She swayed forward slightly onto her toes, watching Mama emerge, examining her sister like a true believer in a divine moment. Then Dorothy rocked back, regained her balance, and started slowly toward Mama.

Mama walked too, straight to Dorothy, and I fell back to watch. Neither spoke. With unblinking eyes, they advanced toward each other in slow old lady steps. When they got toe-to-toe, trembling and mute, the sisters leaned in, their foreheads resting together like brain-conjoined twins. As they wrapped their arms around each other, foreheads glued, Dorothy said, "I love you." They looked out of the tops of their eyes at each other, their contented faces awash in tears.

Hardly able to collect herself, Mama mumbled, "I've missed you . . . terribly . . . all these years, Dot." She sucked in a deep enough breath to say, "I'm . . . so sorry. I love you. Do you forgive me?"

"Shush now, Ella. You're home. Don't worry about being forgiven anymore." Dorothy stepped back a bit and gave Mama a gossamer sweet kiss on her lips. They lingered a moment, their eyes closed as if in a first kiss. When they moved back, the two wrinkled women's eyes shone, a flush of color risen in their cheeks.

Mama stretched her hand out for me to come. She stood steady then, the take-my-medicine worry on her face replaced with wonderment. Dorothy turned to me with a soft smile and I smiled back. Would she hug me too, Mama's black daughter? Or was I just the escort to bring my mother to her? Mama took my hand. Then Dorothy reached over and took the other, squeezing it hard.

"I never thought I'd see my sister again," she said. "How can I ever thank you?"

"You're welcome," I said, squeezing her hand back. She put her arms around me, and we hugged too.

Dorothy introduced Mama to Tony, who'd waited, motionless and watchful, all this time. As he came forward, his keen eyes smiled. "I'm glad to know you, Ella. You and Dolores are welcome here. All right now, let's go on home." He was a man on task, the one in charge of this flock. He'd perfected the role raising four daughters and being the only male in the house.

The two sisters, one thin and one stout, were lost in talk as they ambled through the corridors, oblivious to newsstands and eateries on their way to baggage claim. Tony and I followed, making small talk about the trip and watching them.

"We've been pretty nervous about coming out here," I said in my gentlest voice.

"I know, so have we. But lookit them two," he said, fetching our suitcases off the moving belt. "Now, I just bet they're going to try to talk about every single thing that happened the last thirty-six years in this one week. I think Dot's planning on it."

Tony guided us out to the curb and into the car. While Dorothy talked a mile a minute from the front seat, Mama watched along the route for the buildings and areas she recognized. Dorothy narrated all the changes in town from decades gone by as Mama leaned forward and talked to her through the gap by their doors.

We wound down a thoroughfare, passing the midsized downtown of an urban Indianapolis being revitalized from the impact of rust belt decline and the apparent white flight. Dorothy pointed out all the buildings the city fathers had put up in recent years. Mama craned her neck to see the new convention center, and the I-65 highway that led to their old neighborhood. That was the road that caused their old home to be torn down. We headed out of the city into an area where houses sat on lawns and land, finally arriving in Dorothy's town of Greenwood. That semirural suburb of houses was nothing like the sardine-lot, fifty-year-old houses in the city where we'd lived. Mama, ever the gardener, admired the beds of blue hydrangeas and red geraniums while everyone avoided the scorched earth of her thirty-six years in hiding.

I wasn't looking for flowers. I was looking for people of color. But there wasn't a one, anywhere. Not just no blacks, but no Hispanics, Asians, or Native Americans. It was a world tilted out of balance, skewed to all white. Was that the way the Boehles wanted it? Were they way out here to get away from minorities, like our neighbors in Cold Spring did when we moved onto Florida Street?

In their newish ranch house, we entered an airy living room that opened to a veranda overlooking a patch of green farmland. The home-made quilted decorations and jars of vegetables put up in mason jars announced a midwestern life I'd only read about. Like our old house, they had three tidy bedrooms, including a twin-bedded guest room where we'd sleep. And they had a second bathroom, something Mama never had.

We women went out on the canopied veranda for lemonade. Tony changed into overalls to work the fields with the John Deere equipment sitting out there. I asked him if you'd call his place a farm. Not like it used to be, Tony told me, when he and his brothers kept cows, chickens, and crops enough to feed their families.

"I don't know a thing about farming," I said. "Did your girls work outside too?"

"Naw, they mostly helped their ma put the food up. Except the time Antoinette, our oldest, had to deliver a calf all by herself." She was the only one home when the cow began bellowing, so his daughter stuck her arm inside the cow, all the way up to her shoulder to ease the calf out.

"Antoinette had blood ever'where, all over herself," Tony said. "But we were sure proud of her, being a teenager and all." The cow and calf came through fine.

Urban creature that I was, I couldn't imagine doing any such thing. The closest I'd ever gotten to an animal was feeding lettuce leaves to our pet rabbits who lived in the back hall coal bin that supplied our potbellied stove. This life the Boehles had was more *Little House on the Prairie* than any place I'd lived. New York, DC, and Boston were crowded, multicultural centers of rushing people whose farm contact was limited to a cellophane tray in a grocery store.

The Boehles talked with an everyman speech, stripped of the code switching I used every day in New Jersey to survive. I had the unfiltered street slang, the self-protective black posturing that fended off haters, and the white corporate speak expected in professional settings. Mama warned me not to bring the latter home to the ghetto because it sounded like showing off. If I wanted to make a connection with my Indiana family, I had to drop all those voices and just speak plainly. From the heart, like Luther told me.

As Dorothy prepared dinner I looked at her photos on the walls and tables. Each of their four daughters' wedding photos sat out, in Catholic churches or receptions, perhaps in the parish hall. Some of the cute grandchildren pictured were blonde or blue-eyed. And every one of them in this family gallery was, of course, white, something I'd never seen. Mama followed; her awe evident at the first sight of the family love that her sister said would be ours.

Dorothy reached for another picture, a special one she'd laid out. "This is for you to keep, Ella."

"Here are your grandparents," she told me. "This is your blood grandmother. Your mother's mother. You know we're half sisters because we had different mothers, right? Look Ella, you were a little thing." We peered at the five-by-seven black-and-white, laminated over the frame.

"I'd just about forgotten my mother's face," Mama said, holding the frame reverently. "After she died, I used to look at the moon and see her face watching over me. But then after a while I couldn't remember how she looked. What a treasure, Dot."

My mother was maybe four, with a bowl cut and a fancy dress that covered her knees. She sat between her father in his vested suit and her mother in a long, high-necked dress, around 1913, Mama guessed. I searched Henry and Florence Lewis's features for clues as to who I was. He seemed tall, though he was seated, had dark hair combed straight back, and a pronounced nose unlike any of ours. My grandmother's delicate skin was offset with deeply waved hair braided and curled into balls behind either ear. I tried to feel them, to be a part of them. But nothing connected. Not until my grandmother's eyes drew me in. She looked directly into the camera, full of strength. Her look was like my mother's and my eyes in our own high school portraits. And I knew it, this white grandmother was a part of me.

We ate baked chicken seated in kitchen chairs that swiveled and filled in get-acquainted stories as twilight neared. At the end of the meal Dorothy turned sober. "We're just sorry your Charles couldn't come out this trip. You know he was welcome, too." I wondered if she would really welcome the black man who took her sister away.

"Well," Mama said. "He wanted us to have time alone first, but he's looking forward to seeing you another time." She must have rehearsed that. I felt badly for Mama, because I knew she'd sanitize her secret—that the man she gave up her family for had been an alcoholic for much of their marriage. He'd functioned for the most part, working every day, and drinking only at home. But still, here was my mother hiding it from

My mother, Ella, with her birth parents, Henry and Florence Lewis, circa 1913.

her sister with the familiar charade we played outside the family. Mama had been clear she didn't want me to say anything about it.

We were polishing off our chicken when Mama cleared her throat. "Uh, tonight while it's just us, can we talk about when I left back in '43? Pick up the pieces?" She wiped her mouth with the napkin, twice.

"All right, I'm glad you want to," Dorothy said. "I do too."

This is why we came. If Dorothy had any long-brewed bitterness toward Mama or racist remarks about Daddy and me, it would come out now. A pain jammed my mostly dormant old stomach ulcer, and Tony's eyes focused on Mama. Dorothy cleared the plates and set a box of Kleenex in the middle of the table, where the salt and pepper sat.

"Dot, can you understand that Charles and I were scared to death to stay here in Indianapolis?" Mama started. "People were so prejudiced, we were bound to get hurt. I wanted to get married and have a family like everybody else. But who here was going to marry me after I divorced Alan?"

"Charles gave you a family, but," Dorothy opened out both palms, "why didn't you talk to Dad before you left? He might've understood, Ella."

"But not Mother. You know she wouldn't have it. Remember how she refused to let Tony, my first boyfriend, in the house because he drank beer and drove too fast?"

"I surely do," Dorothy said. She told us he'd found the perfect job for his wild streak, in a pit crew at the Indianapolis Motor Speedway. A natural fit for the boy riding Mama on the back of his motorcycle, outpacing cops who chased them down alleys. Dorothy said Mama was some hot ticket in her day, sneaking out on dates and waking her up when she climbed over Dot and into bed late.

One look at the expression on my face and Mama started laughing. "You talk about fun! We used to slip out and go hot-rodding around in his roadster too. A 1929 cream-colored dream! I even rode on the hood one time, posing like Miss America on a float. But we hit a bump and I fell forward off the car. It was lucky I fell between the tires, because he couldn't stop in time. The wheels rolled right past me on both sides."

Dorothy got up and went to her bedroom to get a newspaper obituary. Mama chuckled as she read how Tony became a riding mechanic and a crewman at the speedway, with his picture hanging on their wall of fame. "And Mother said he wouldn't amount to anything," Mama said, as she and Dorothy giggled like teenagers.

No wonder Mama married a black man in Klan country. She was a rebel all along.

15

INDIANA CHRONICLES

The family hadn't known what to think when Dad didn't hear from Ella within a couple of days of leaving Indy. He called long distance to the girlfriend she was supposed to visit in Worcester, Massachusetts. But she hadn't heard from Ella in years and didn't know anything about her coming to visit.

The Indianapolis police came over to talk with the family. They asked about Ella's state of mind when she left on the train. Was she nervous or scared? No, Ella was looking forward to a vacation. The officer questioned Dorothy, the little sister who might know what the parents didn't. Had Ella confided in her? Maybe she was running away? No, Ella had been fine as far as Dot knew.

Dad told the police to question the ex-husband because of the divorce. Or maybe she'd gone back to that hot-rodder Tony, the one she wanted to marry before Mother put the kibosh on it. Between Mother's consumptive coughing spells, she suggested the woman Ella rented from. "Dad's hand shook when he handed the police officer your picture, Ella," Dorothy said.

Dad hardly slept during those days, dragging himself to work, while Dorothy sat beside Mother's bed, praying the rosary, until the police called Dad to come downtown.

Sitting across the desk from Dad, the officer said they'd cleared all the people mentioned and checked at Holcomb's but had not uncovered any leads or signs of Ella around Indy. So the search had started in Worcester. The Massachusetts police interviewed the girlfriend who was supposedly hosting Ella. His daughter hadn't been to her house, nor to the city or state as far as the authorities could tell. Ella wasn't in any of the nearby hotels or hospitals.

"She's in New York," Dad said, handing the officer a postcard. Dorothy had found it that same day, the hotel postcard from Ella in their mailbox. Dad told the officer that Ella must have stopped in New York along the way. She was having a time seeing New York and sent her love.

The police contacted the hotel, but Ella was gone. So, the New York City police opened a missing person's report and began their own search. And there was something else: the police said since Ella's train went from Indiana across Ohio and New York, her case was now considered an interstate concern. The FBI had been called in.

They confirmed that Ella's train made all its scheduled stops without incident along the entire route. They would make further inquiries to see if anyone had seen her at those stops. But they were racing the clock, because Ella had been missing several days, which made it more unlikely they'd find her.

Dad said as her father, he had to do something. So he boarded the same train Ella had taken to New York to find her himself. When he arrived during rush hour, Grand Central Terminal and the madness of Forty-Second Street overwhelmed him. Though he knew nothing of huge cities, he made his way to the Times Square hotel from Ella's postcard. But she wasn't registered. He insisted the clerk check in the back office. Yes, she had been there, and the police already knew she'd checked out days ago. Paid her bill and disappeared out into the crowded street, like all their guests did every day. He roamed the streets, hoping to see her at some bus stop or restaurant, but didn't.

He asked the NYPD to let him go with them door-to-door, showing Times Square shopkeepers Ella's picture, but they couldn't allow it. They checked hospitals and morgues but did not find any trace of Ella. Not her; not her body. When an NYPD detective sat Dad down and rifled through Ella's file, he shook his head. The sad truth was that several hundred girls went missing in New York City every year, he said. They're victims of rape, kidnapping, and murder. Some are forced into the sex trade or sold into white slavery. He looked Dad in the eye and said New York was no place for a well-brought-up girl to come alone. He was sorry, but the case was closed.

"We are declaring your daughter a victim of foul play," the detective said. "That's not murder, because no body was found. But we can't do anything else, unless there's new evidence."

Dorothy's story hurt to hear, as I imagined Mama's father stumbling out of the precinct alone amid impossibly tall skyscrapers. His daughter disappeared into nothingness like the steam rising from the subway grates under his worn-out shoes. I hoped he had let out some feral cry.

Back home, Dorothy went on, Dad was met with hysteria. Dorothy and Mother spent their days rehashing the investigation. Was Ella really dead if there was no body? Where did they have white slavery? Was she taken out of this country? Couldn't somebody check further? Dad contacted a private detective, but the price was out of the question—they already barely had enough to cover Mother's medical expenses. There was nothing else they could do.

The house sagged with grief. Dad said there would be no funeral if there was no body. There was no more listening to favorite radio stories. No more playing with the dog. No more outside jobs to supplement their income. No more light in Dad's eyes.

Dorothy woke up about 5:00 AM that first Christmas to the sound of Dad sobbing and moaning such as she'd never thought was in any man. She waited a while, hoping he'd stop. But when she finally went to her parents' room, Dad asked over and over, incoherently, what happened to his wonderful girl. Mother sat wrapped in her wool blankets in the side chair, coughing up thick yellow phlegm in that room where the shades were never raised. They stayed in that tomb the entire day, not knowing if Ella was dead on this, her favorite day, or living in shame in some God forsaken place. Dad never got up. Not for coffee, not to open presents, not to eat dinner. By six o'clock that night, Dorothy said, she'd gone back to bed, relieved to make Christmas go away.

Mama's eyes were fixed on her lap. "I feel so small knowing how I hurt you."

I was hollowed out, too. The anguish Mama had put them through was the pile of hurt Luther warned me I'd set off when I went looking for them. It made me ashamed too. We sat at the Boehles' kitchen table writhing, each in our own way, from the wound Mama had made and the scab I'd torn off it. Yet I wondered if she had ever worried about how her family would be devastated when she disappeared.

Like some saint, Dorothy answered, "Ella, God answered my prayer and sent you back. I love you no matter what."

The sisters petted each other for several minutes, Mama repeating her humble contrition while Dorothy lovingly pardoned her. How could my aunt be so forgiving? Her response was so foreign to the acting out and arguing David, Daddy, and I would have done if this kind of drama were happening in Buffalo. That's what I had feared would go on here. But we weren't in Buffalo. Here there was no carrying on, no raised voices, and no accusations.

Hearing the Indianapolis side of the story and the world Mama had erased put my mother in a new light. She had been a reckless young woman joy riding on the back of a motorcycle in the 1920s and '30s until her mother put a stop to it. Then she was a Catholic divorcee in the 1930s and the runaway wife of a Negro in the '40s, when it was a social abomination. But had she ever considered the consequences for the rest of us? Had she ever considered the long view? Had she gone into my father's black arms because she was naively color-blind? Did she ever see the hurt that would come to her family as a result?

"And what about your kids' lives, Mama?" I wanted to say. What about the sort-of race her reinvented life left my brothers and me to figure out? David tried to be the blackest of race advocates while Charles Nathan was on the white side of town where his porcelain skin could pass. And I straddled the racial divide, studying and practicing white ways to be accepted in white corporations while dying to rip off the mask and be black me. We three kids were caught in the middle of two races, although our parents had assigned our lives wholly to the black one. Mama had always thought race shouldn't matter. Yet we siblings were fossilized in the amber of our parents' decision to mix races and hide at a time when 96 percent of Americans were against it.

Yet I loved Mama dearly, something that would never change. As she and Dorothy leaned into their embrace, I realized Mama never had any idea of what she was getting into when she married Daddy. By coming to Indy, I stumbled into my younger mother, the one I never knew existed.

In our bedroom, Mama took off her wig and slipped on her nightgown. I asked if, during all those years, she'd ever thought about contacting Dorothy. After the antimiscegenation laws were changed by the Supreme Court, had she thought of trying to get in touch with her family or bringing us all together?

"Not at all," she said. "I'd been married to your father twenty-five years when they changed those laws, and we had you kids. I closed that door and learned to live with it. Do you think I could just turn up in Indy with a black man and three colored children?"

The next morning both sisters came in the kitchen looking as if their mother had dressed them alike, in floral sweaters and pastel pants. Dorothy poured rich-smelling coffee in the mugs waiting on the plastic placemats and brought out a box of old-fashioned cake donuts—plain, heavy ones. She and Mama each took one and, at the same time, broke them in half and dunked an end into the coffee, the same way Mama had done for years in Buffalo. Before the second bite, they touched their donut halves together like a champagne toast and dunked again.

Mama looked out over the back field, like she didn't want to face Dorothy when she asked how Mother and Dad had died. Of course, she knew consumption killed Mother and a heart attack took Dad, before either of them turned fifty. But, did they suffer much?

Before Mother died, she was bone thin and bedridden. Dorothy quit college to tend her in the bedroom, kept roasting hot against her chills. Mother couldn't take even baby spoons of puree or bouillon. Rather, all her thin energy was used struggling for breath. Each time she tried to suck in air, a mass of phlegm that sounded thick as sludge pulled up through Mother's chest. It traveled a half inch or so, then dropped back down in her upper cavity. Settling in. Thickening. Clogging her airways.

"You should know what her last words were," Dorothy told Mama. "She said, 'I wanted to see Ella before I went.'"

Mama's mouth fell open. "She said that? Why, I didn't think she loved me."

"Oh, she surely did, Ella," Dorothy said. "Mother did love you."

The confounded look on Mama's face bore out her belief that her stepmother only loved Dorothy, her natural born daughter, not Ella, her obligation. Had there been so many miscues between stepmother and stepdaughter that they had misspent their lives together? So many that Mama had yoked herself to an unfounded resentment for sixty-some years? Believed she and Daddy could never make peace with Mother because she didn't know Mother loved her?

After Mother died, Dad moved in with Dorothy and Tony. He piddled around on little electrical projects occasionally, only perking up a bit around Antoinette, a toddler at the time. He survived the loss of both wives and Ella for only two more years before he too passed away.

Dad was dressed in his good suit and laid out in the casket when Dorothy put a rosary in each of the side pockets of his jacket. One was Mother's and the other was Ella's. The family gathered for a private viewing at the undertaker's, saying prayers with the parish priest before others came to pay respects.

All the while people were coming with garden bouquets and kind words, Dorothy listened above the din for Ella's voice. But she didn't hear it. Once the place emptied out, she went to check the guest register for Ella's name. It wasn't there.

Dorothy asked Tony to take Antoinette home and let her have time alone with her dad. She put a folding chair at the head of the casket for herself and an empty one at its foot. She waited in silence several hours into the night, having made it safe for Ella to come when nobody else was there. That way, she wouldn't have to explain herself to anybody. Ella had been Dad's favorite, so Dorothy expected her sister to show up if she was still alive. But she never came.

"I thought we'd sit, the two of us alone with Dad," Dorothy said, reaching for Mama's hand, "before he was gone forever."

Dorothy went back in the morning, to check the guest book again to see if Ella had slipped in. But neither Ella's name nor any other name in Ella's handwriting was listed.

At Dad's gravesite that morning, Dorothy took the first fistful of dirt and threw it on the casket down in the grave. Then she threw a second. That was her good-bye to both Dad and Ella. "I knew you must be dead. It wasn't possible you were alive and hadn't come for Dad," Dorothy said.

Mama broke down into mourner's tears like he'd just been lowered into the grave. By the way she buckled over in her chair, she must have felt both grief and shame. My own eyes misted for the grandfather I never met, and for Mama's anguish, soaking into the wet tissues she squeezed with fingers bent from arthritis.

"I'm glad I didn't know he died back then," Mama said. "It would have been miserable not being able to come home. He stayed healthy in my mind all these years, thank God."

"Would you like to go to the cemetery and see them?" Dorothy asked.

In a half hour we were in the car, looking for a florist. Mama bought a fresh bouquet tied with a white ribbon, and Dorothy drove straight to the place where their parents were buried. Mildred and Henry Lewis lay side by side in a grassy double plot marked with a joint grey marble headstone. The air was thick with the smell of freshly mowed grass. A nearby tree blew gently in the bright morning sun, casting shade over Mama's stony face. She laid the flowers midway across the two graves.

"Will you pray with me?" she asked.

We stood on either side of her, reciting the Our Father and the Hail Mary for the parents who raised my mother. My white people.

As Mama prayed, my quickened heartbeat confused me. I hadn't expected to feel anything for these dead people. They'd only been names to me. "Idiot," I thought, understanding my white ancestors had been good people, parents devastated over losing their precious daughter. Their pull from the grave brought a growing sense of connection. The mutual love we shared for my mother came over me. That bond was undeniable. I owed these white grandparents my honor.

16

THE GUARD TOWER

We drove back to Dorothy's house to meet her daughters that afternoon. There was a schedule set up, as Mama requested, so she could meet them one at a time and not be overwhelmed. While Dorothy said her girls were excited to meet us, I wondered if my cousins would be as open to me as they were to Mama. Just because Dorothy and Tony seemed accepting of my blackness didn't mean their kids would be. Dorothy got her sister back, after all, but those daughters might not have a stake in their black cousin. With a lifelong barrage of white mistreatment behind me, I couldn't muster the wide-open trust Mama was ready to give them. Instead, I sat up in my guard tower, ready to be pleasant but watchful for any weasel-waffling, to see whether we wanted to be related.

First came Toni-she, as they called Antoinette, to distinguish her from her father Tony. The eldest, she was a thirty-something with a mane of black curls who lived next door. Later, Judy, the vivacious youngest with spiked hair and her husband in tow, came through the door kissing and hugging both Mama and me. They surprised me, because our conversations were easy and open. As if Mama and I were the relatives they had been missing.

"This is the most beautiful moment," Judy said. "You two have made us so happy."

Darlene came last, with her two little blonde girls. She was quieter than her sisters and very Midwestern-nice. She gave us an invitation to come see a show at the country-and-western lounge she owned with her husband—an invitation for us to be seen out in public, as her guests. Mama's eyes sparkled. She was all for a night on the town with the local cowboys. My little hunched-over mother, who called rock 'n' roll noise, was excited to go to a honky-tonk. Maybe she wanted to relive the heydays she and Dorothy had revealed earlier.

But while the invitation was generously offered, it made me uncomfortable. I never listened to country music, something black people associate with the racist South and rednecks. Weren't the southern country singers from the states that had never gotten over the Confederacy losing the Civil War? Weren't they the ones with the Confederate flag on their shirts and porches to signify their love for those good old slavery and Jim Crow days? Indianapolis was the former headquarters of the Klan, and I worried about the leftover haters who I suspected were in plain sight around town. Probably neither Dorothy nor Darlene had thought of that, since race was never a part of their lives. But what would I do if Darlene's bar was full of those flags and songs about the beauty of pure white girls? That kind of fear had forever kept my radio dial turned away from "country" everything and my feet safely marching away from such places.

However, after all that afternoon's talk about kids, houses, schools, church, and jobs, I had to admit that none of my white cousins seemed to give a gnat's eyelash about my race. After the last one left, Mama, Dorothy, and I sat in the living room. While they discussed dinner plans, I pretended to watch TV as I drew inside myself.

The way the whole family tried to make Mama and me comfortable rattled me. I still couldn't believe that they were opening up their one-hundred-percent white world to me. It couldn't be that simple, could it? Like our country hadn't been through race riots and federal troops escorting little black kids into white schools. Like people hadn't tried to deny me an education or burned a cross on my lawn or tried to consign me to a sort-of, invisible life. I held back, feeling the prejudice I'd carried on my back for thirty years. Careful to respond appropriately to the casual warmth offered, I wasn't sure if I could let it all go and let them in.

Later in the week, Dorothy and Mama sat on the light blue and mauve sofa watching *As the World Turns* when they decided to make a surprise visit to their cousin Vivian. They'd been childhood playmates all those years ago, and Mama thought it would be great to see her again. Dorothy and Vivian kept up sometimes, but she hadn't told her about Mama resurfacing or coming to visit Indy.

After dinner, in the twilight, we drove over to another part of greater Indianapolis to Vivian's. The sisters chattered about the things they all did together as girls as Dorothy drove. They laughed, wondering excitedly if they'd get away with a fast one or if Vivian would recognize Mama with no prompting.

She lived in a white wood-frame house on a quiet working-class street. A small light was on when we pulled up. Mama and Dorothy arranged themselves side by side in front of the door for maximum impact, and I stood behind them. Dot rang the bell, and they elbowed each other in anticipation.

After ringing twice, Dorothy knocked. We waited on the front porch a little longer. Finally, a woman opened the door a crack and peeped out, her thin lips as hard set as plaster. In her cotton housedress, she studied Dorothy first, who said hello nonchalantly, part of the little ruse. The woman shifted her eyes to Mama, who looked back expectantly. Vivian did a quick double take at the sisters. Then she punched the door open and her eyes popped wide at Mama.

"Ella, where in the hell have you been?"

I watched as the tired-looking woman put a foot forward, her hip slung into the door to hold it open. Before Mama could answer, Dorothy stepped aside and gestured to me with a smile. "This is Ella's daughter."

I moved forward and took Vivian's limp dishcloth hand. It was hard to tell if she wasn't used to shaking hands, as some women weren't, or if her response was something uninviting. I suspected the latter, since she didn't say anything to me.

Vivian remained listless, said she couldn't invite us in because her husband had gone to bed early and she didn't want to wake him. It was late for her, too, and she was about to go to bed. Mama smiled weakly. Without ever offering her missing-person story, which Vivian obviously had no interest in, she was the first to say good-bye and head down the stairs. I heard the door close before we got to the bottom.

"No more surprises, Dot," Mama said, holding up her finger in a warning.

Dorothy and Tony took us to a cafeteria across town for dinner later that week. As we waited our turn to be served, the all-white clientele lined up: men in open collars and hands in their slacks pockets, a man in overalls with his family, a teased-up blonde flashing her prom queen smile at a man speaking with a twang. The servers called me ma'am, the way people had in Louisiana. I got back in my guard tower, ready to defend my out-of-place self in this rural white world. I clenched my hand and released it over and over, waiting for that racial comment or gesture made just for me, the only black in sight.

We put crispy fried fish and steaming chicken potpies on our plastic trays and went through the crowd to an empty table with a checkered tablecloth in the middle of the dining room. We bought one of their huge strawberry shortcakes, with its suspect red goo holding the berries together over a sugared biscuit, like Mama made. After the hot food, we scooted up to the table with our four forks to dig into it together.

Our interracial family sat together, right out in the open, talking over Jimmy Carter, gas shortages, and when the summer corn would be ready. We sipped coffee and scraped red goo until it hit me that there was nothing awkward between us. I was having a good time, without the undercurrent that always ran through me around white people I didn't know or trust. What we cared about at our table was our own fun and nobody else. Out in that restaurant crowded with customers, not one person looked at us, or cared who we were or what was going on at our table. Surprised as I was not to be treated as an outsider, I couldn't explain how that could be true. But it was clear I needed to understand it.

When we got back to the house in Greenwood, as everyone was taking off jackets, I just said it straight out. "Can we sit down and talk? It's about something I hope won't spoil our reunion."

"OK," they agreed, automatically heading to their places at the kitchen table. Dorothy looked quizzically at Mama as she turned on the light and removed the plastic place mats. Mama shrugged her shoulders when she thought I couldn't see her, signaling Dorothy that she didn't know what I was going to say. Mama wasn't going to like it, but if I didn't speak up now, I'd go home without knowing if we fit as a family.

They sat waiting for me to speak while the round wall clock seemed to tick-tick-tick too doggone loud. With the taste of fear on my tongue, I broached what had, and maybe still would, separate us.

"Can we talk about race? None of us can afford to ignore white and black issues after what happened to this family."

"OK," Dorothy said. "Maybe it's time we did."

I intentionally didn't look at Mama, whose disapproving eyes I'd already caught a glimpse of. We hadn't discussed me dumping my life's baggage in the middle of her redemption week, but Mama had such a different take on race than mine. She took it in stride and approached it in common sense terms, without the emotional outrage Daddy, David, and I did. Like how she said people were just people, and all that racist foolishness was ridiculous. Like how she never talked with us about pride in our mixed heritage. Like how she said the civil rights movement was black people's business, even as she had a black family sitting right in front of her. Like how she'd let her own white blood be nullified by the black-only box my brothers and I occupied.

But race was my business. Ever since I was transformed by my Howard experience of black power, it always had been.

I sat on the edge of my swivel chair, so my feet touched the floor. "See, I've been discriminated against by white people all along. So, it's important that we be open about race. In fact, I came out here with questions about you, relative to who I am."

Mama cleared her throat. I kept looking at Dorothy, whose eyes were calm and kind.

"What kind of questions do you have?" she asked. She folded her hands, resting them on the table.

"Well, how do you feel about black people in general?" I asked.

Dorothy hardly knew any. Both she and Tony had worked alongside a few blacks, her as a nurses' aide and him at the GM factory. They were decent people. But after work, they went to their black families and neighborhoods, and whites went to theirs. They didn't socialize outside of work, but they all got along and got the work done.

The idea was foreign to me, them living their whole lives without any black relationships. They'd just stayed in their white world, physically and emotionally detached from the continual struggles black people, including me, had lived in. Could they ever understand what we had been through? Would they ever really see us for who we were?

"But you live in this state where the law used to forbid intermarriage," I said. "Where my parents had to run from. How do you and the family feel about that kind of thinking?"

"Biggest damned fool law I ever heard of," Tony said. He tapped his pipe on the table edge, struck a match, and puffed the tobacco in its bowl. They had never even known about that law. Probably because nobody they knew ever fraternized across races. Or because no black news ever appeared in the mainstream newspapers they read. But yes, Tony said, Indiana did have prejudiced people back then and yes, now too. Of course he'd heard about the Klan and some of what they were capable of. Tony looked me in the eye. "But that wasn't ever part of our life. That's not what we believe in."

"So then, how do you feel about my mixed race?" I asked. "My real question is whether I am seen here the same way as Mama. Because I'm not white."

Mama folded a napkin into smaller and smaller triangles, fussing to ensure all the edges aligned. She didn't look up.

"Oh, Dolores," Dorothy said, leaning toward me. She opened her hands. "Your race is not important. You are our niece, period. We love you every bit as much as your mother."

"We don't care about any of that," Tony said. "What we do care about is family. We have always wanted to have everybody together, including the girls' in-laws and their families, distant cousins, and now you."

"Even though I consider myself black?"

Dorothy said she could see why I wanted to clear this up, and maybe they didn't understand race the way I did, but she did not want race to make any difference among us. "We'd love you if you were polka dot," she said.

That was the answer I hoped to hear, of course. But as sincere as they seemed, I could only hope they wouldn't hurt me, even if unintentionally. Confusion wormed through me. Would my wholehearted embrace of this white family be selling out my race, or be complicit in taking my light-skin privilege to a higher level? This was all new ground. Being half white in this sense was something neither American society nor I understood in 1979.

"Well that is great," I said, with a smile on my face and a softer tone. "But what about my father and Luther? They're darker, not light like me and my brothers. Do you accept them too?" I didn't ask but wondered if they were willing to be seen in public with obviously black men.

Mama abandoned the napkin that was beyond further folding and rubbed her temples with her fingertips.

"Yes, of course we accept them," Dorothy said. "Because they are your loved ones and are part of the family too. That's why you're here. There's nothing more important than your being part of the family, all of you."

She told us the story about when she was twelve and Mother told her Ella was her half sister, because they had different mothers. She was devastated, thinking that separated them somehow.

"I cried all day, because I wanted Ella to be my whole sister, just like I want all of you to be my whole family. Now I know that halves and steps and blacks and whites don't count in this family." She came around to me, and I stood up to hug her. We had been strong enough to look into each other's worlds and speak honestly. And now we had arrived at a meaningful understanding. I went off to bed relieved, with a genuine affection for them.

In our twin bedroom, Mama sat in the armchair unlacing her orthotic shoes and rolling down her knee-high stockings. As she rubbed her hammer toes, bent up at the joint, she looked up over the tops of her square glasses at me. "I didn't like you bringing that race stuff up, Dolores. The way you were questioning them as if they're not sincere. I was wondering if you have forgotten that racism goes both ways? Or if you saw that you were part of that."

I asked her what she meant.

"Black people were mean to me because I'm white, too, you know. But we can't lay the misdeeds of some at the feet of everybody else, and you know it. Why would you question the Boehles like that after they've opened their hearts and home to us?"

"Let me explain."

She kept right on talking. "Remember the black conventioneers who refused to stay with us because I'm white?"

I did remember that hateful hallelujah woman in the pink feathered church hat that had a hissy fit about Mama.

"It still hurts me to remember her insulting me in my own home, simply because of my race. I don't want even a whiff of that here. You're not to press Dorothy and Tony any further about race. How could you do that in their own home? Here they are making a way out of no way and you question their integrity. The very *i-dea*."

Mama tugged her nightgown over her head, wiggling her stiff shoulders to get it on. "Even though some black people mistreated me, I don't go around suspecting black people who are kind to me." Her voice quaked. "I expect you to be bigger than that. She invited you here."

"I didn't mean it like that, Mama. I'm sorry if I handled it wrong, but you don't know how worried I've been about this. I didn't want to set myself up and get hurt later."

I felt lower than dirt. For all my degrees, I hadn't known how to determine the humanity of my relatives in some better way. Being dressed down by Mama was like being seven years old again, facing the kitchen corner for talking back. "Nice girls are polite," she'd told me so many times.

I was still awake long after Mama fell asleep. Each of her open-mouthed snores rattled loudly at the back of her nasal cavity, making sleep impossible. Worse, my twin-sized bed was not next to a wall I could lean against. It made me nervous I'd fall out in my sleep like I'd done at other people's houses. So, I bundled all the bed covers around me in a nest on the floor. That's where you got the best sleep, according to Daddy, who often slept like a baby in the middle of the living room floor after too much beer and baseball.

Laying on my back in the dark, I turned over what I knew about family love. In Buffalo, Grandma was the only family member who loved us without reservation. My little family of five had long accepted the fact that many other black relatives excluded us from their daily lives and celebrations. The close extended family experience these Boehles seemed to live was only somewhat replicated by our made-up, mixed-race Clique Club family. There our unacceptability was accepted. Because they, like us, were people with poor or no relations with their blood families based on their unthinkable black and white family makeup. The Boehle family's open acceptance and bloodline loyalty existed on a different plane from the fragmented, conditional, catch-as-catch-can family relationships I knew.

How could I live my white people's offer to love one another when even my nuclear family had such a long a history of running away instead of fostering kinship? Mama ran off with Daddy, leaving her family to think she was sold into white slavery or some such evil. Charles Nathan secretly joined the army and ran away to serve the morning after high school graduation; when he came back from Korea, he ran to a white wife on the other side of town. I ran off to college and far-flung cities for jobs without a thought of going home. And Daddy ran into his Four Roses bottle so he wouldn't be present when he was.

There on that bedroom floor, I considered whether I even knew how to connect, let alone with my white family. And, to be honest, could I release my all-black identity and give my white half a real life? Was that what my roots search boiled down to?

Headlights from a passing car shone in the window and Mama snored on. I sat on that guest room floor and saw a familiar figure in the room. My boogeyman lurked on the opposite wall. The one I'd given my life over to so long ago. The one whose warning burned like a Klansman's cross every time racism blocked my path. He'd taught me that whites could not be trusted. That I had to be ready for whatever grief they might gin up for black people, because they always did. He was not only my truth, but every African American's protector and boogeyman. The one who kept us on alert and saved us from being surprised when whites hurt us.

We sat there together in my white people's bedroom. I'd held that boogeyman's hand ever since that white cab company wouldn't come to take my four-year-old self, burned on the potbellied stove, to the hospital. I'd let him run my life ever since.

And now with a white family who believed race had no part in the love we could share, I had to decide whether to let them in. It meant putting my boogeyman out.

As I tried to tuck the tangled blanket under my cold feet, finally, it came clear. My identity and what life to live was my own choice, not society's or the government's or my boogeyman's. I could choose to expand my identity to fully embrace my white heritage and love my white family or let my own prejudice keep me in an all-black box.

I looked over at Mama, asleep in her bed next to me, and saw the exemplar of knowing who she was while loving both races.

———

Our last night in town, Dorothy, Tony, Mama, and I went to Darlene and Wayne's country-and-western nightclub, The Outside Inn. They met us at the front door and showed us to a reserved table with the best view, situated away from the stage where revved-up partiers were rocking to a live band.

Waitresses hustled drinks to a good crowd, some wearing cowboy boots and bandanas at the neck. We ordered beer all around, and Mama was laughing it up after a few sips. The all-white crowd danced steps I didn't know to the band's somebody-done-somebody-wrong songs. I felt like a certified shape-shifter being in such a place. If it wasn't for the family invitation, I wouldn't be caught dead in a country bar for fear of rednecks. But Mama and I were special guests in a club where people were simply enjoying themselves. My boogeyman and I looked the place over closely while Mama and Dorothy talked, but we didn't find a single Confederate flag. Nobody called for "Dixie" to be played; there were no good ole boys looking for trouble. When Darlene came by to check on us, Mama and I complimented the successful business she had.

When a familiar slow tune started, I caught myself easing up. My white family brought us out for fun, so I clapped along as they did. A couple danced romantically around the perimeter of the dance floor, the young woman's face resting on the broad chest of her partner. Mama gave me a soft smile. I was glad she couldn't see inside me, the narrow-minded one who had stereotyped this place and these people without reason.

With the romancing couple in front of me and the loving family beside me, I climbed down out of my guard tower. These relatives had no problem with my blackness. They had done everything to show me love, and I'd be a fool not to accept them. When I smiled into Dorothy's happy face, the tension in my muscles released. I did have room inside for my white heritage. I did have room for the family love offered. There would be plenty good room for all of us to mix and meld.

I smiled back at Mama, who had joined the crowd in singing that familiar song. Now that she had drunk her rare half glass of beer, she raised her arm in the air and shouted, "Yee-ha!"

17

SHIFT

Aunt Dorothy's fifteen-page letters, cards, and calls started right away. They were the communiques that helped us grow closer despite the distance. And most important, there were some short, cordial conversations between Dorothy and Daddy, as I remember. Theirs was the one essentially healing connection that would help us understand some of the trickiest parts of our relationship. But the opportunity to put Daddy and the Boehles together was forever lost when Daddy died a few months after Mama went back to Indy, before the Boehles could ever meet him.

While Daddy lay in a coma for weeks, everyone came to the hospital except David. When I tracked him down at a friend's house to go to the hospital with me, David choked up.

"I can't stand to see him wired up to everything but the kitchen radio," he said. No, he wouldn't look at the respirator pumping air through a tracheotomy cut in Daddy's throat. No, he couldn't bear to relieve Daddy's scabbed tongue with a glycerin swab. Not his father who'd become his drinking buddy, the father he did the *Amos 'n' Andy* routine with, the father who came to David's sixth-grade classroom every year with a stalk of sugarcane and a ball of cotton to tell the inner-city have-nots about farming down south. In adulthood, David was more like Daddy and much closer to him than Charles Nathan and I. At the graveside, he was the one who broke down, holding the wide-brimmed white hat he bought over his eyes but unable to hide his sobbing behind it.

The rest of us had had far more complicated feelings about Daddy for a long time. Mama, married to him for thirty-seven years, looked lost, and Charles let out a yelp of what?—anguish, guilt, or love?—over the casket. But even as I mourned him, I still had not come to terms with all the damage his Four Roses whiskey in that pink plastic cup had caused among us. As a teen, I'd childishly tried to stop the drinking by pouring his bottles down the drain. Of course, he had other bottles hidden and a liquor store two blocks away, so his hair-trigger rages continued to turn our home inside out. Before going away to college, I resorted to staying in my room to avoid interactions when my brothers were out and Mama was at work. And as an adult, I only tolerated him.

Yet Daddy handled his business. He was a faithful husband and father who came home every night to preside over dinner. He guided, disciplined, and entertained us kids. He was a solid provider who for decades took three busses across town in Buffalo blizzards to get to his welding job.

Mama did her duty as wife and mother while wringing her hands and urging Daddy to calm down for nearly forty years. Pleading for Daddy to stop raging at all of us, pleading for him to stop hitting us with that welding shop strap with buckles on the ends.

But we were all clear on our unspoken pact—to keep up appearances and keep outsiders in the dark about what went on at home.

In the week after his funeral, Mama and I pulled up in front of a takeout to get some dinner. She put her hand on my forearm, to stop me getting out.

"You had such a hard time with your father," she said.

"What tore me up was what his drinking did to our family."

"You're not the only one," she said. "I disliked Daddy's drinking as much as you. But I was married 'for better or worse,' and did my best even when times were at their worst."

We sat in that hot car in front of the pizza shop, finally confessing our shared misery of living with an alcoholic. Like the canceled plans and cover-up excuses when Daddy was in no shape to go out with Mama. Or the Thanksgiving dinner when he drunkenly passed out in his stuffing and gravy in front of company. Or on Charles Nathan's graduation night when he tried to knock his son out for signing up to join the army. What we didn't know then, but I learned years later in an Adult Children of Alcoholics meeting, was that Daddy's kind of chaos went on in many families and impacted everyone in them. But none of us ever knew to get help.

This was the secret Mama wanted buried with Daddy. It was for this reason she did not call her newfound and loving sister Dorothy to come for her husband's funeral. We all agreed it made no sense to arrange Dorothy's first visit with black people while we were being gutted. Nevertheless, Dorothy showered Mama with flowers, letters, and calls of concern in the months that followed, loving her as only a sister could.

Meanwhile, we Jacksons burrowed in together, to dredge up and weigh the racist assaults that drove Daddy to drink. And as he finally rested in peace, we privately acknowledged that liquor was the only escape he found while defending his white wife, his mixed children, and his own black body during a lifetime when America thought we were an abomination.

Mama and Daddy's twenty-fifth anniversary, 1968.

———————

Later that summer, Mama and Dorothy wanted to see each other again and insisted I had to be a part of their plans. They both came to visit Luther and me in New Jersey, which became their pattern for the next twenty-six years, to vacation together, usually with me. It was broiling hot the week they had their second visit. We wandered a mall worshipping its air-conditioning, then went home at closing time. The house was still intolerably stifling.

With the only air conditioner in our master bedroom, Luther dragged in twin mattresses from the guest room where Mama and Dorothy were staying. Dressed in our thinnest clothes, the elders climbed into our queen bed while Luther and I lay on the floor mattresses. As that old air conditioner, set on blast, chugged on noisily, our German shepherd whined outside the bedroom door.

"He's hot too," Mama said, getting up to let him in. He plopped down near our feet, in the line of cool air.

"Good night, Mama," Luther said.

"Good night, Dorothy," Mama said.

"Good night, Luther," I said.

"Good night, Dolores," Dorothy said.

"Good night, Baron," Luther said.

"Good night, John Boy," Aunt Dorothy said, laughing at *The Waltons* show sign off.

During that visit, I got out the genealogy chart that had triggered my search for Dorothy, hoping we could flesh out more of Mama's family history beyond her parents. Could they trace the line back to my European who came to the States, the equivalent white root to the African Aunt Willie told me about? Finding my African had anchored the family line that was lost when slavers severed those ties. Maybe with a similar white anchor I could also understand the essence of the whiteness in me. There had to be more beyond the current day Boehles and my grandparents Lewis.

Over several days, the sisters set about piecing stories together through fuzzy memories and family lore. It took a lot of sorting and backtracking through the folks best remembered before they decided my family was French and Scotch.

We crafted another genealogy tree. But once it was laid out on paper, we saw Mama was wrong. She was talking about her adoptive grandparents' heritage, not her birth mother Florence's bloodline. In fact, she didn't know anything about Florence's background, except she was nicknamed Ella after her own mother Ella, and both those women had died young. When Florence's mother died, her father (whose background Mama didn't know either) arranged Florence's adoption by George Scott, a paper hanger who immigrated from Scotland, and his wife, Ella Amanda, who had French heritage.

But they were not my bloodline. My only palpable connection on Mama's side was all those Ellas, who gave me my own never-used first name—Ella.

On my grandfather Henry Marshall Lewis's side, both his father, Charles Lewis, and his mother, Minnie Knowlton, were born in Ohio. Where *their* elders came from was unknown, but the names had origins in Britain, Wales, Scotland, and Ireland. Minnie was a member of the Marshall drugstores family, and her dad was a banker.

The story Dorothy and Mama told me about their father's family amounted to this. Minnie died young, and Charles Lewis remarried. He and his second wife, who had more children, had already cut Henry off because he decided to marry Florence, who they thought beneath their station. During summers when Mama was a girl, she went back to Ohio to visit her plain-living grandparents, the Scotts. They would dress her in her best for the occasional dinners she was invited to at grandfather Charles's big three-story house, with the music room, grand circular stairway, and her three aunts and uncles. While once wealthy, the Lewises apparently lived beyond their means for so long they later had to convert second-floor bedrooms into accommodations for four boarders. But they held on to their symbols of better days, and still set the table with china, linens, and the crystal napkin ring that Dorothy pinched the only time Henry's second family was invited to their house. Fifty years later, Dorothy gave that napkin ring to Mama. Now it sits in my dining room hutch, my only other connection to those white forebearers.

I'd only found two generations back on my white side, with some probability of bloodlines near Britain, but had not found my European root. What I did find was that my discovered whiteness, adopted and related, was so much more privileged and freer than I or my black family began with. My maternal grandmother was raised by a striving craftsman who chose to immigrate to America for a better life, plying his trade freely in the late 1800s while my black sharecropper grandmother was being raped by a plantation white man. My paternal grandfather Lewis was a self-made electrician hired to help wire up the Indianapolis Motor Speedway, and his grandfather was a banker born in 1852, when my black people were slaves. My grandfather Henry grew up in a fancy home where his parents' status made them think they could look down on other whites while my black father feared Klan violence by all classes of whites. Yet the kind of opportunity privilege my white people had didn't flow to me through my mother. She gave it all up for the love of a black man, and I was raised never knowing what that meant.

But Mama did pass down a certain whiteness to me—her knowledge of what was on the other side of the color line. However incidental to her practical mothering, she gave me her own Standard English and white social manners. She used the entitled sense that one *could and should* ask for what was important from those who could change things (like getting my fellowship funds transferred to Harvard), something many blacks were reluctant to do. She lived the assumed right to be unapologetic for who you are despite other's opinions (even as blacks tried to hide their ways to accommodate white's expectations, like I did when shape-shifting). Mama gave me insight into the white Catholicism that helped me understand the Boston jobs and political landscape dominated by Irish Catholics while I lived there. And she gave me the understanding that white people *could* have the decency and respect for other races that she and her sister shared.

Not until I wrote this book did I understand what my half-black, half-white, mixed race meant. My early struggle to rise to my full potential as the black person I knew myself to be was advantaged by my insider's notion of how some whiteness functions in America. That unique mix of determination and insight was its own form of privilege.

At seventy years of age, I picked up the hunt to find more about my makeup by spitting into an AncestryDNA kit. Yet when the test results showed my heritage was 75 percent British Isles and northwestern Europe, I went into orbit. How could I be that much more white than Mama's 50 percent donation? It had to be that old Georgia plantation rapist's blood I never wanted to claim that ran through me still. So, my black half, the half that defined most of my life, is only a quarter of my biology.

American society said I was Negro at birth, and I was raised to understand myself as black. It was not only Mama's white blood that counted for nothing back then, it was all my white relatives who were erased from my tree. In this land of the one-drop rule, born of this country's obsession with keeping "white" at 100 percent, my black identity outweighed 75 percent of my biology. So how should I define race? Culture or biology? Nurture or nature?

———————

Luther had a bout of lupus later the year that Aunt Dorothy visited us in New Jersey. It destroyed his kidneys, the first of his vital organs it would attack. He began life-saving dialysis three times a week that cleaned out accumulated toxins and fluids, wreaking havoc on the benefits of his medications, as they were cleaned out every other day too. During this upheaval, we became pregnant for the first time in our eight-year marriage. The news brought out the most joy Luther had ever expressed.

Jennifer was born in 1981, a child so white looking I couldn't tell which baby was mine among the white ones in the hospital nursery. We thought it was my white heritage that made her that complexion, but a black woman pointed out the brown tops of Jennifer's tiny ears as her natural color. Sure enough, our daughter morphed into a brown child. Jennifer was a precious brown baby born into a different world than we'd known, into an extended white and black family that claimed and loved her from the start.

Luther, Dolores, and
Jennifer, 1981.

It had been two years since Mama and Dorothy reunited, so they
planned another visit, this time in Buffalo to meet Charles Nathan,
David, and their families. While on maternity leave, I would go too, and
introduce the baby. But the difference in our black and white worlds
drove a debate among us Jacksons about where they should stay.

"They can't stay here at the house," Mama said. "They might be
scared in the ghetto around all these black people. What if they act like
Angela's sister did that time she came to Buffalo?"

"That woman musta been scared the black would rub off," David
said. He thought if Dorothy stayed with us in the 'hood, we'd be sure
she was OK with black folks. But Mama said it was too much. I don't
know what excuse Mama used for not extending the hospitality of her
home, but she booked Dorothy and Antoinette in the Holiday Inn on
the white side of Buffalo.

To create just the right setting for the family to all meet, Mama
wanted us to all go out to dinner on their first night in town. But our

family rarely went out to dinner because of the cost, so nobody knew where to take them. One night at work she talked it over with her white nursing supervisor, who suggested a waterside restaurant with a private dining room.

At the restaurant, the hostess showed Aunt Dorothy, Antoinette, Mama, me, and the baby in her little seat past the lively happy hour to that private room. There we found David and his girlfriend, Clarissa, and Charles and his wife, Gee, dressed up and waiting for us. As Mama introduced each one, Dorothy leaned in and kissed them warmly. The aunt and cousin who had embraced me showed the same love to each one of them. Her "I love you" was so heartfelt, so simply honest, it seemed as if she had always been one of us.

The setting was lovely. We sat around a large wooden table, surrounded by soft white lights strung through lattices and vines. The privacy of the room made for conversation we could all join in, and the opportunity to speak freely. As Mama presided over the union of our black and white family, the most beautiful thing in the room was the blissful glow in her eyes. It was her dream come true, watching them lean in over their plates, getting to know each other and weaving our colors with love into whole cloth.

The next morning, David drove them over to the house for coffee and Mama's cinnamon coffee cake. As we milled around the kitchen fixing our coffee, Mama showed Dorothy her Buffalo Bills football game tickets under a refrigerator magnet. She and David bought them every year along with community bus tickets to the stadium. She loved eating BBQ with the crowd while somebody else did the driving.

Not to be outdone, Antoinette said their Indianapolis Colts would be way out front of the Bills, and Aunt Dorothy rattled off their players' statistics like a sportscaster. They had a favorite sports bar where the family went together to watch the Colts over burgers and beer, she said.

Those two old ladies gave tit-for-tat, their version of trash talking about who would be in the playoffs and have a chance at the Super Bowl. Raising the ante, David and Antoinette traded phone numbers so they could rub in insane plays and victories after game time. By the following season, the two of them were traveling to attend Colts-Bills games together, hosting one another in Buffalo or Indianapolis. And on a future visit, Mama and I went to their packed sports bar to see the Colts play on a bewildering number of wide-screen TVs.

When the football talk died down, we sat at Mama's dining room table, which was dressed in the good white tablecloth, special blue glass plates, and a peony bouquet from her garden. As we settled in, Angela arrived, her hair freshly teased into a white bouffant. She was still Mama's best friend from forty years in the Clique Club and was the last of the old gang still in Buffalo. Mama introduced Angela as her other sister, the one she'd been through it all with.

I served slices of that mile-high coffee cake while Angela told how she and Mama had raised us kids like cousins, especially me and her daughter Sandra. It was true. I was godmother to Sandra's son and could hardly remember a special occasion without them.

"Angela was the heart of our fun," Mama said. "Her house was full of parties when the kids were little, and she organized our families for more get-togethers than you could shake a stick at."

They had so much more than fun together. The two of them made the shower favors by hand when both Sandra and I got married, cooked dinners together for church fundraisers, visited every Christmas, and cried together after their husbands died.

"The whole nine," Mama said.

Dorothy studied the woman who had filled her sisterly shoes the thirty-six years Mama had been missing. "I'm grateful you had each other," she said. "It's a blessing to know you."

Angela reached across the dining room table and took both Mama's hand and Dorothy's. "You two don't know how lucky you are, getting back together," she said. Her eyes were weary when she turned to Dorothy. "My white family doesn't know about my black family. They're so prejudiced, I can never tell them. I have to live a lie, a double life."

This was old news to us Jacksons, and I think Mama must have already said something about it to Dorothy. But Antoinette's lips parted, and her eyes flared momentarily, bearing witness to how little the unini-tiated understood mixed-race life.

Those two women would meet again. Some years later, Mama was found in the morning, unconscious in her evening bath, the water turned cold. A neighbor noticed she hadn't taken her morning newspaper in and called David. Mama had had multiple seizures sitting in that water all night long.

Angela and Dorothy sat together in Mama's hospital room. Their mutual devotion to her brought them there faithfully every day until I could fly in. Then they mothered my frightened self and stayed on when I had to go back to work. Sandra, who worked at the hospital, checked in with the staff every day on Mama's care. After Mama came around and Dorothy went back to Indy, our constant Angela never missed a day beside my mother, sitting sentinel until she was released to rehab weeks later.

Five years passed as Jennifer grew, Mama and Dorothy kept up, and Luther tried to make it through work, despite his continual decline from lupus. Then, in May 1987, he was found dead in his hospital bed, his heart destroyed by the unfiltered residues deposited by the dialysis that was only so effective. He was forty-five. I was thirty-nine. Fourteen years after we met, Luther was gone.

After six years of deacons praying over him, new doctors, changing medications, waiting for a transplant and clinical trials, Luther died quietly in his sleep. We had not been able to fix him. I had believed we could.

I took five-year-old Jennifer to the funeral parlor for a private view-ing. We stopped in the dim light of the foyer before she saw what she did not expect. She had gone to the hospital with Luther some Saturday nights, their dinner packed, storybook and games in tow. She saw the blood from his body cycle through transparent tubing and back into his vein. She heard the alarms when his or somebody else's blood pres-sure went haywire. She saw the dialysis chair he was strapped in flipped upside down to keep him from fainting. But she had not understood.

"You know Daddy has been very sick for a long time," I said as we stood in that foyer.

"He is? You didn't tell me."

"He was sick, and, well it got so bad that Daddy died, honey. We came here so you can say good-bye to him."

"He died? Daddy died? That's not fair!" she cried. "Everybody has a daddy, but now I'm not going to have mine?"

Mama didn't ask the Boehles to come to that funeral either. But she was right at my side, the best person to help me. I had been very stressed for some time with Luther's illnesses, my too-demanding executive job, and raising my little one. She knew I could barely cope.

As a single working mother, I spent the next three years just putting one exhausted foot in front of the other. All the house, yard, taxes, bills, teacher conferences, entertainments, and parenting responsibilities I'd shared with Luther were now mine alone. But the hardest part was when Jennifer tried to make sense of her little life. She couldn't remember her father's face, so I put his picture next to her bed. She questioned if the dark circles under my eyes would ever go away, or was I sick like Daddy? She burst out sobbing in the movie when a mother bear was killed. She begged me not to go to work and leave her.

It escaped me then, but functioning independently caused me to grow, to trust my own judgement, and become self-reliant. With the help of a live-in babysitter and Mama's helpful visits, in a few years, I came to live life on my own terms.

18

EUROPE

Ten minutes into my carefully detailed presentation to a German colleague in my vacationing boss's absence, he interrupted me. "May I ask you a personal question?" he said.

Confused by what seemed inappropriate, I looked up and said, "What is it?"

"Are you prepared to come to France and work for me?"

"To do what?" I asked.

He swirled his fingers in a circle over the charts I was showing him. They gave an explanation of how our company did its planning for the American market.

"This," he said. He needed somebody in the company office on the Riviera who could do what I did but for the global market. He had just been appointed worldwide VP for the whole business in all countries and was building a new team. Would I join him?

I'd visited a few other countries for pleasure, but living abroad? He promised a raise, a visit to meet the team, and a look at schools and housing before giving my final answer.

Six weeks later, Jennifer and I moved to France, a few miles from the azure blue Mediterranean Sea, between its coastal cities of Cannes and Nice. I rented a mountainside villa on a tiny road with black olive trees and a riot of pink bougainvillea in the garden. In the first few days we enjoyed alfresco dinners and a view of pink-orange sunsets on its large veranda. All that beauty and sunshine began to lift my veil of depression, and this black girl began to dream again.

Jennifer started in the village public school as a French-as-a-second-language student. A former au pair came to live in again, and once the French authorities had Mama's eighty-year-old fingerprints and the police affidavit showing no criminal record, she was approved to come to France with us. And I began as worldwide operations manager for a $2 billion business unit of my tech company.

Mama had never been to Europe, but once she got to work in our flower garden and became familiar, the neighbors and restaurateurs in our village would call, "Bonjour, Grandma!" She would stay for a month or three before going back and forth to Buffalo.

As Mama grew more adventurous, we went over to tour London Bridge and Buckingham Palace with Jennifer. And on another of her visits to the Cote d'Azur, Mama asked to go to Rome, especially to see the Vatican. She proved a real trooper at her age, riding overnight in a sleeping train car and throwing good luck coins over her shoulder into the Trevi Fountain. At St. Peter's Basilica, she used her most hurried steps to keep up with the tour guide showing us the Vatican Museum jewels and priceless religious tapestries. Finally, she climbed to the Sistine Chapel to admire Christianity's story as Michelangelo painted it on the ceiling.

Naturally, after Mama became more comfortable in France, Aunt Dorothy made her first trip to Europe to vacation together as we had done in the States. She packed Dinty Moore Beef Stew and cans of tuna, so she didn't have to eat unfamiliar food in the gastronomic capital of the world.

I showed them the Riviera's beaches by the sea and the highlights of old town Nice. We drove the twenty-five miles to Monte Carlo to see Princess Grace (Kelly) and Prince Albert's castle. Later in the week we drove over the border into San Remo, Italy, for market day. We strolled by the tables and racks one wasn't supposed to touch until they came to a cheese seller. In a ridiculous charade of sign language and a mixture of French, English, and Italian, we tried to find out what types were offered, the weight in kilograms versus pounds, and the price in lira, francs, and dollars. It took fifteen minutes of laughing to buy a wedge from the hefty lady with a forest growing under her arms. She moved the knife to a much wider slice than we asked for, probably to make the transaction worth her wasted time. Or to take advantage of American tourists, the worldwide sport.

We walked on to find a scenic place for lunch. Once seated, Mama and Aunt Dorothy went to the ladies' room. When they didn't come back for a long time, I went looking for them. They were still closed in their individual stalls, sitting in the dark, laughing.

"What are you two doing in here?" I asked. "I was getting worried."

I punched the light button, which is usually on a timer in Europe to save electricity. Because they were elderly and slow, the lights had timed out before they finished.

"We can't do anything in Europe without you, even go to the bathroom," they howled.

Back at my house, Aunt Dorothy asked if we could go to Paris. The Riviera was nice, but she'd hate to come to France and not see Paris. So, I took nine-year-old Jennifer, my seventy-something aunt, and my eighty-something mother to the City of Lights, serving as tour guide. The supposed four-person hotel room was jammed with a double bed and two roll-out cots. With all of them opened out, there wasn't an inch anywhere to walk to the bathroom. Jennifer crawled over closest to the window, then me, then Aunt Dorothy, then Mama, in order of who could climb over the most people to get to the toilet during the night.

On a Gray Line tour bus around the city, they kept their seats while oohing and ahhing through the window at the Louvre, the Opera House, and the Eiffel Tower. But when the bus stopped by Notre Dame Cathedral, they stood up to collect their things and get off, without any discussion. I followed them as they wobbled inside the sanctuary, humble missionaries come to experience their Catholicism in this most famous place. Other tourists admired the gothic flying buttresses and frightening gargoyles, but my family wanted to get inside to pray. Even though Mama had been excommunicated forty years before for divorcing and remarrying, her face was the picture of devotion.

In that dark medieval sanctuary with its immense stained glass rose window, the crowded mass was celebrated in French. I listened to the hunchback's bells ringing outside in the tower and meditated on the pungent smell of the incense burning, picking out the few words I understood. Afterward, Mama exclaimed, "We knew when to stand, kneel, and sit. It's the same mass as in English. Let's do it again."

"Oh yes, let's do it again," Aunt Dorothy said.

Jennifer, who was learning to speak French quickly in school, translated the sermon for them, pointing out words for God, communion, and prayer so they'd get more out of it the second time through. As we talked between the masses, I noticed that nobody was staring at our mixed group the way people did in America. The French routinely cared less about our race than I did, a phenomenon that had already begun to free me. For the several years we lived in France I was treated like and felt more like a wholly accepted person— more than being the black person perceived by judgmental white Americans ever had. It was this foundational sense of belonging that Jennifer absorbed during her formative years and carried through her later life in America.

Mama and Dorothy seemed transfixed in the sanctity of Notre Dame, where maybe all of us thought God was closer than in our small congregations back home. The four of us held hands during the sermon they now knew the gist of, ushering me into the family devotions they had grown up with. Experiencing their kind of Catholicism together was a naked intimacy for me that brought Mama's roots sharply into focus.

After we moved back to the States, we had constant calls and letters with the Boehles, but the best times were our visits. We traveled to each other in Buffalo, Indianapolis, Florida, New Jersey, and Massachusetts. That constant feeling of belonging together grew into a new life of laughs, support, and unconditional expectation of more.

Mama (left) and Dorothy tell their story of loss and redemption.

Mama (left), Dorothy, Dolores, and cousin Judy in Florida.

During those years we talked about our race and cultural differences openly, then blended them into a communal understanding of who we were together. But since Mama had never talked about what being Midwestern meant, it wasn't until twenty years in that I got an insight.

That was when Antoinette took Jennifer and me to the Indianapolis 500. The family wanted us to have the full race-day experience. It started with gifted tickets and breakfast at an in-law's, served on a checkered flag tablecloth with Speedway logo napkins. We learned who set the pole for the race, how to watch pit crews blaze through tire changes and gas ups, and who was favored to win.

The stadium, a structure that seemed to rival Rome's Colosseum in size, seated almost a quarter of a million people around its oval. We got there early enough to see the beehive of pits and crews just inside the track's edge before the green starting flag swooshed down and the cars took off.

As the famous drivers and flashy cars roared by with a deafening cacophony that hurt my ears, I saw something equally amazing in the stands. Most of the fans swung their heads around with the pack of cars speeding by at over 220 mph, and kept quiet. There was only an occasional gasp or audible crowd reaction when someone crashed or pulled ahead. Fans peered at the board to see what lap the drivers were on and stayed in their seats rather than standing and blocking the view from behind them. The amazing orderliness and civil behavior of their Midwestern manners were the opposite of East Coast fans who screamed vulgar names at athletes or fought each other drunkenly in the stands. Those civilized racegoers reminded me of my even-tempered mother. Her own sensible behavior was all over that stadium.

As I interpret that Midwestern nice, at least in my family, it must have been part of the respect for people and patience for difficult situations that Mama always demonstrated. It must have influenced her to step out and marry a decent man who happened to be black. It must have been the part of Aunt Dorothy that allowed her to take Mama back without recrimination. It must have enabled Dorothy to see only her sister's needs when she came to David's funeral.

Our shining black prince died of a heart attack at fifty-three, and it took Mama to her knees. I found her crying at the assisted living home, so distraught she couldn't talk. Behind closed doors, she collapsed into me as we cried together. David was the best of our community, a jive-talking inner city teacher who knew everyone in the 'hood and who helped create Buffalo's Juneteenth Freedom Festival. My righteous brother had taken such good care of Mama. He made it abundantly clear that his white mother belonged to the black community and brought his friends to help care for her after she was widowed. That had kept her safe and woven into our old black neighborhood when she lived on her own, the last white person on the block. Now, she had to bury him.

Aunt Dorothy came immediately. She took up her post next to Mama, to mourn with her and comfort her, as Mama leaned into her like a lost child. Dorothy stayed for days and days, taking turns with me—listening, holding Mama's silences sacred, and helping her cry.

Our reunited family was the lucky one. We held onto the healing bond others in our mixed-race Clique Club family would not enjoy. When Angela, Mama's Clique Club sister-friend of fifty years died, Mama called me, just as I changed clothes after work. She sounded as torn up as a blown-out tire. "I'm furious," she growled, something I'd never heard in her. "Angela insisted on taking her double life to the grave."

Before Angela passed away, she made her three adult children promise to honor her dying wish. She was to be buried back in Smalltown under her maiden name in the plot with her white family. She told Sandra and her brothers not to come to the funeral and blow the cover off her secret black life.

"Whenever I think about how cruel she was," Mama wrote in a note to me, "to abandon her children, I am so low down . . . disgusted . . . disappointed—however low, I'm it."

How could Angela betray her kids after Sandra spent years taking her to the emergency room and a million specialists' visits? How could she, after living in Sandra's house for decades?

What I didn't know, Mama said, was that Angela's white family had worried about her bad health and wanted to look after her back in Smalltown. Angela told them she'd hire live-in help in Buffalo instead. That "help" was her daughter, Sandra. When Smalltown called, Sandra answered her own phone in her own house, posing as a paid Negro caretaker.

I kicked my shoe off so hard it landed in the back of the closet. Sandra was my lifetime friend. My Clique Club cousin. "Did you talk to Sandra? She must be so hurt."

Sandra told Mama, "We had her in life so they can have her in death. I never met those people and don't care to know them." They held their own service for Angela at the parish she attended; Mama and a few friends joined the family.

But Sandra's middle brother let it all hang out. He later told me, "We had her wrapped in a sheet of plastic and shipped her to Smalltown, like she wanted. And we didn't even go to our own mother's funeral," he said.

I didn't know which mixed marriage horror story was worse. Was it Mama's, living in hiding from her family for thirty-six years while they thought she was dead? Or was it Angela's, living a double life, lying to her whites and denying the black family she lived with, even in death? One thing I wasn't about to say out loud was that both Mama and Angela deluded their families in order to have the men they loved. But clearly neither had understood what those unions would do to us mixed-race kids. We had been expected to brush off our parents' unfathomable absurdities like no explanation was needed. I'd fallen right in line, like it made sense, never considering I must have had a white family for thirty-one years. Such was the suffering American society wrought in families that crossed segregated battle lines in the mid-1900s.

Mama and I talked about how all the Clique Club women had to give up their family relations after they married black men. Like Sallie, whose brothers shouted "*Fangue!*" and declared her dead after she married a black man, despite his elegance and good technical job at Sylvania. As Sicilian immigrants fighting the surge of hate against them trying to be white people in America, they said Sally had drug them back down to the bottom. For her treason, they never acknowledged or spoke to her again. An old neighbor called years later to let her know her mother died. When she tried to join her brothers at the casket to pray, they walked away. There was no seat for her at the family table during the funeral repast.

And what about Marie, whose family pretended her black husband, the band leader at the most successful jazz club in western New York, didn't exist? Family invitations to weddings and parties that came addressed only to Marie and her daughter, Diane, all had to be declined. Marie would not go without Bill.

"None of your friends have the kind of peace you ended up with," I told Mama. "None of the others got the love of both families. Angela's way of dealing with this mess was dreadful. But maybe you can forgive her. Everyone in your family forgave you."

"I'll try," she said limply.

What I can tell you is that we Jacksons and Boehles had twenty-six years together before Dorothy and Mama passed away in the early 2000s. Whether we sat in the yard talking about recipes or attended first Antoinette's wedding and then David's, or walked by the Seine in Paris looking for Dorothy's hamburgers, we knew we belonged together. During that journey our understanding of family ties and values bloomed bigger and brighter than I could have hoped when I went to find the Boehles.

19

BELONGING EVERYWHERE

We moved back to the States where Jennifer finished eighth grade at the local public middle school. But after the rigors of her private French international school, our public school had fewer classes at her level. She was fluent in French by then, something too valuable to lose. Jennifer had gone to that private school because my company offered to pay for education of expat children in schools where they could keep up their native English. But now that she was going to high school, we had to decide where she would go.

We visited two private high schools recommended by black friends whose children attended them. To send Jennifer to such a white environment would be going against Luther's prior refusal to consider private schools.

He had good reason. At the age of three, she went to a preschool in New Jersey touted for its stimulating program. In a converted old mansion, teachers led educational activities and documented Jennifer's progress in regular written reports. We were well pleased, until the day I dropped by unexpectedly. When I opened the heavy wooden door, loud James Brown music filled the foyer. Several young white teachers had Jennifer and Clarence, the only other black child, dancing as they egged the kids on to wilder movements. The teachers clapped out the rhythm, pointing to the children and laughing at them. No white kids danced in this minstrel show. The white people I paid a fortune to train and protect my child had turned her into a ridiculous darkie to entertain themselves. Yet they were surprised when I demanded they stop, then laid out the headmistress and them. That institutional racism made up Luther's mind. It proved to him that most whites, even if well meaning, self-declared liberals, cannot or will not see or cop to their part in keeping black people down.

Later, when a private elementary school approached us about enrolling Jennifer, Luther refused to consider it. Pulling on his short beard, he said public school had been good enough for us, and it would be good enough for her. She would be comfortable there. He wouldn't risk his baby being mocked or mistreated as the only black kid in a hoity-toity school like that. She'd lose her black culture. Then what black man would marry her, he asked. Because certainly no white one would.

It was important that Jennifer knew where she came from, so I worked hard to steep her in black culture and history, even as she lived in white environments and loved her white relatives. We talked about how the civil rights movement won African Americans unprecedented access and opportunities, a point often revisited when we entered hotels, libraries, and restaurants. She celebrated African family and community values during Kwanza. We attended Jack and Jill's curated events for black children raised in white environments, and Jennifer sang in the children's gospel choir at our black Baptist church. On our way to France, we went to Senegal and visited Gorée Island. That scorching white-sand outpost, the largest slave trading center on the West African coast for four hundred years, horrified my nine-year-old Jennifer, and me. It turned our stomachs to see firsthand how our ancestors were held and shipped out in chains to become slaves in the Americas.

Knowing who she was and being able to maneuver in white spaces served her well when faced with discrimination. When a racial slur was slung at her during sleepaway camp, she twisted the boy's arm behind his back until he apologized, while other campers cheered. I cheered too when she told me about it, because Jennifer stood up for herself when confronted with the trouble every black person knows is possible. She just had to work on using words instead of physical assault.

In the end, I thought Jennifer could handle going to a private (read *white*) secondary school. She was strong academically. She certainly knew how to function in white environments, having lived with white kids in the suburbs and in France all along. She was a beautiful, polished girl with a great transcript and a million-dollar smile. She was bilingual and was also familiar with Ebonics, having grown up with some Buffalo family that spoke it. Jennifer applied to two top schools and got into both.

At the first parents' weekend at St. Paul's School, she took me to see the other black students who competed with her for scholarships and introduced me to others. Some of those black girls from another scholarship program later called Jennifer an Oreo—black on the outside, white on the inside. Probably the real rub was some jealousy about her friendship with a boy from the 'hood, over which a few of the girls threatened to beat Jennifer up. But Jennifer *was* different from them. As I saw it, her time living on the Riviera, her white friends, her spot in the ballet company and King's English weren't black enough for some of them.

They were girls like I had been; diamonds in the rough whose academic success had won them a place in an elite institution. They clung to community among their own, just as I had at Harvard, because I didn't fit in the mainstream, and wasn't sure I wanted to. For me, black friends were essential to survive, and I think that was so for these girls too. You had to line up with the all-black-all-the-time or be deemed a sellout. Sadly, those same girls Jennifer introduced me to at parent's weekend later crossed the street rather than speak to her. If my father was still alive, he might have called that another instance of "equal opportunity racism," blacks hating on their own for not staying in their prescribed box.

Jennifer went on to Brown University, where she embraced everything that was in her and reached for so much more. She studied history and did musical theater. In concert with the Africana Studies Department she stomped out African dances to urgent drums in a tattered slave dress, then tap danced in a production of *A Chorus Line*. Fascinated with other cultures, she did a semester abroad at Al Akhawayn

University in Morocco. And from that experience she went on to Princeton, did research in Algeria, and earned her PhD. While there she worked alongside a dean to prepare minority candidates to make their PhD applications as strong as possible.

I taught my African American daughter that she was entitled to try everything, that she belonged everywhere she chose to go despite anyone who said differently. That's what personal power looked like to me, building on the hard-fought gains and experiences of her black and white family, to reach for whatever she chose.

Jennifer made me proud, the way she embraced these ideas. Yet her approach to the world of privilege was nothing like mine had been. I had clung to other blacks while trying to survive the foreign world of Harvard's power and whiteness. Instead, Jennifer went through the Ivy League assuming her place with friends from all races, religions, and socioeconomic backgrounds. Unlike the carefully crafted public masks I had put on in white environments at her age, Jennifer is her same self with everyone. It had never occurred to me, all those years I tried to give her the best of the striver's ambitions Harvard had imprinted

Mama and Dolores with Jennifer at her college graduation.

on me, that she would become so much more facile at navigating such an advantaged worldview.

After graduating from Princeton, Jennifer taught African history to a largely first-generation college student body at City University of New York (CUNY) in the Bronx and Harlem. It was the same university her father, a first-generation student from Harlem, graduated from with an engineering degree.

When she started that position, Jennifer found out why she had been selected over other candidates from Ivy League colleges. During an interview, she had mentioned a summer college job she had picking produce on a farm in Norway with a migrant worker from Central Europe. In a turn away from professional internships, she wanted a completely different experience and place.

Jennifer loved being outside by the glistening fjord backed by green mountains. But that migrant farming proved to be hard work. She slept on a cot in a barracks and squatted until her knees ached picking strawberries in long low rows or climbed ladders and reached until her shoulders were sore picking cherries off trees. For ten hours a day, in brutal sun and pouring rain, and under the night lights if the crop was too ripe, she did her business in the fields because there were no toilets. When she got back, her main advice for me was to always wash produce carefully.

Two generations before, her black grandparents had worked southern cotton and tobacco fields for a living. When I told my elderly mother-in-law in North Carolina what Jennifer was doing, she replied, "You said what? She pickin'? I thought you were sending her to those fancy schools up north so she wouldn't have to."

And yet, that subsistence life experience had influenced the CUNY faculty to choose her for the professor position. Some thought she would better relate to the hardships of the nontraditional, largely first-generation student body at CUNY.

Jennifer knows how most African Americans struggle regularly with job and wage discrimination, inadequate and unaffordable housing, health disparities, police harassment and shootings, food injustice, racially motivated misconduct, insensitivity, and inhumanity. While she has not had to face such strife in her own life, she knows her many privileges were won through our own family struggling against that very list of inequities. Like all our country's non-white minorities, we both know that simply having brown skin can not only block any opportunity but also bring about grave harm.

I taught Jennifer she belonged everywhere because that was my own belief and goal. In addition to holding onto my beloved black community, I went for jobs, friendships, and residences that spoke to my broadest interests and opportunities, sometimes where few other blacks were to be found. For years, certain black friends have wondered how and why I wasn't living in the 'hood and socializing exclusively in the black community. Some of them never socialize with whites.

"Why you wanna live over there in that white neighborhood?" a black professional friend asked me. Without waiting to hear how I loved access to the subway, banks, jobs, and ready amenities available around the corner that are harder to find in the 'hood, he told me nothing could beat living among his own, where he was fully accepted. He wouldn't dream of putting up with trying to get along with white people in his private life, even though there had been multiple homicides in his neighborhood, one a block from his house. There, he didn't have to edit his cultural tendencies, see people cross the street in fear as his son approached, or be ignored by neighbors who acted like he didn't exist.

Another friend said it like this: "A white man in my bed? Not gonna happen. I need the comfort of brown skin next to me. Somebody who knows and loves my culture like I do."

The black skepticism about the way Jennifer and I live no doubt comes in part from racist hardships they know about, the ones we all know are possible, as well as having no loving relationships with whites. While Jennifer and I are surely African American, being shaped by my mother and her white family's example that race should not matter has stretched our view. It's a dream, we know, but the one we hold out for, no matter that I won't see it in my lifetime.

20

FLOW ON

Mama sat in her robe at my faux wood-block kitchen table, her folded up walker resting against its side. It was 2003; she was in her early nineties and still coming to visit me in Cambridge on my frequent flyer miles. She sipped morning coffee loaded with cream, our lollygagging way when we visited. A pleasant breeze floated through the open back screen door that summer day, along with a too-close condo neighbor's inept, one-phrase flute practice.

The homemade rhubarb jam on the table was Mama's favorite, although you couldn't give it to me. She'd stood over my hot stove cooking it the night before, her un-wigged hair thinning to bald on top, the rest frizzled. Specialty fruits were nowhere on the salt-free, fat-free, sugar-free, taste-free diet at the assisted living home where she lived. So, Mama was in her glory, sculpting rhubarb onto her breakfast toast one crunchy-tart bite at a time, with the intention of a jeweler.

She closed her eyes, savoring the last piece. After swallowing, Mama kept still, a bit too long. Then she cast a sideways glance at me, opened her mouth as if to speak, then closed it again.

She finally spoke, saying she had a lot of time in that home to think back over her life. "I've got something to say, and I want you to hear me out." She listed toward me and clam shelled my face in her hands. "It's about how I ran away from my family."

We'd been a normal extended family with the Boehles, at least in our own integrated eyes, for almost twenty-five years. What was left to say after we'd already dissected that story six ways to Sunday?

"I need to make peace with it before I go. It haunts me, in here," she said, patting her heart. "What I mean is, maybe I should never have run off with your father."

Good Lord. This was the first time Mama had expressed such second thoughts. And she was doing it with me. I kept my face neutral, wondering what she was saying. Did she mean she should have accepted spinsterhood and being shunned? That she thought her life was all wrong after nearly forty years of marriage? That her life was a mistake and mine was too?

"What do you mean?" I asked gently.

She clutched a handful of the yellow-and-blue tablecloth we'd bought together in Paris. And as she often did to announce the difficulty of asserting herself, she cleared her throat.

"While I was with your father, I never thought how being mixed could confuse you kids. And even though I knew my family would be hurt by my leaving, I figured they would just get over it. People all around me suffered because of what I did. So maybe I should've never married your father." She was quiet, bunching and releasing small wads of tablecloth.

I took her in. She was one wobbly, near-deaf ancient lady who wore custom-made tan orthotic shoes of two different sizes to hold misshapen bones from falls. My four-foot-eight mother, with sagging skin like a rooster's wattle, the one who could turn her walker like a slow-motion ninja, had a heart as fragile as a robin's egg. I wouldn't hurt her for the world, and here she wanted me to be her truth-teller. Or did she want my absolution? I took a sip of my cold coffee.

"Why now, Mama?"

She said she didn't have much time left. There had been a cancer on her nose, even though the surgeon said he got it all. "We both know I could go any day now."

"You did what you thought was best."

"Maybe your father's drinking was my fault too. He might not have drunk so much and taken it out on you kids if he didn't have to defend our marriage every day." She cleared her throat. "Well?"

I took off my glasses and rubbed my eyes to buy time. She was always saying she wouldn't be on this earth much longer, that every visit might be our last time together. Was Mama making her deathbed confession to me in advance? The one it had taken her a lifetime to say out loud? My mother was asking me—me!—to wash her soul before it was too late. I shut the back door to block out that awful flute playing so I could think straight.

"You don't mean you regret marrying Daddy? Or do you?"

"No," she whispered. "I guess not, but I regret the pain I caused just the same." She looked up, her eyes red.

Who was I to say what she should have done with her life? Buck the antimiscegenation laws to have love and marriage, or accept spinsterhood by staying with her white family? I wasn't about to judge. She'd paid enough, a tiny Atlas with scant shoulders holding up our mixed-race piece of sky. The one who'd kept all of us from being crushed by Daddy's drinking and the country that thought we were an affront to nature and decency.

She deserved the peace her eyes begged for. I told her she should not second-guess what she did. I squeezed her shoulder softly and said she had the same right to the love of a husband and children as the next person. That Daddy loved her more than what he feared he was up against, even when he knew the dangers of marrying a white woman in the 1940s. She pulled her shoulder up and started to say something, but I didn't let her.

"Daddy's drinking was the only way he could cope with the haters. And that was his choice. It wasn't your fault. And you saved the Boehles from a miserable life of ostracism if people in Indianapolis had known who you married."

She scraped up toast crumbs on the tablecloth with her knife, not looking up when its hill of crumbs reached the edge. "You don't think what I did was wrong?"

Everybody makes life-changing decisions and has to live with the consequences. Like the rest of us, Mama needed to be OK with the face in the mirror.

"No, you were not wrong," I said. "You were a good wife. You made it right with Dorothy and you showed us kids how to deal with prejudice. All of us love you so. Anyway, it's America's disgrace, not yours, that you had to run and hide."

She let out a squeak of relief and leaned back. "Thank you."

"Things have changed, Mama," I said. "People see mixed-race differently now. Most would understand your choice. They would fault the racist system in Indiana for what you had to do, not you."

She wanted to talk about how things have changed. "Do you know how many more mixed couples there are now?" I asked. "It's a thing, you know." In her old age and her very small world of assisted living, not only computers and cell phones had passed her by, but Mama had missed the growing acceptance of biracial identities in the aughts. She didn't know people were marrying those of other races in record numbers throughout America, especially on the West Coast and northeast corridor where I live.

I told her the name calling has died down. Bullies used to call me mongrel half-breed Oreo high-yellow blue-veined mulatto quadroon redbone confused nigger sell-out, although some still seem to think that last one applies. We talked about how the mixed-race "look" has become more recognized, so that fewer and fewer strangers try to place me into more traditional identities. Fewer people now ask me if I am black, white, Hispanic, or Mediterranean. However, I told her, when random race tourists still try to examine my skin like a public exhibit and ask some version of "What are you?" I just smile and say I'm from Madagascar.

She fell out laughing. I was using her old response to those who treated us like pariah when we were kids. Back then, she'd smile brightly at their disapproving scowls and say something pleasant like we were all being cordial.

"Do you know what you and Daddy started back when you got married?" I asked. "You guys were the grandparents of America's mixed-race evolution." We talked about how the Lovings were considered the parents of mixed-race because theirs was the marriage that the Supreme Court used to overturn antimiscegenation laws in 1967. But my parents married twenty-four years *before* the Lovings did it. They were old enough to be the Lovings' parents.

I told Mama what that meant in today's terms. For the first time, the 2000 Census offered an option for the mixed-race demographic to self-identify from among scores of races. That allowed me to acknowledge for the first time, legally and honorably, both the black and the white sides of my heritage.

It had been so emotional for me, that after more than two hundred years of counting, the Census no longer dictated that I was black but asked me to define myself. It felt as if my country could finally see me, as did the other 7 percent of mixed-race Americans. Later, between the 2000 and 2010 counts, mixed births would grow three times as fast as single race births, a trend accelerating with more speed than expected. Mama had little idea.

It was late morning, so we got cleaned up and dressed. We were going out into "civilization," her word for mixing with the rest of the world outside the home. She wanted to "gallivant" to the neighborhood seafood restaurant for lunch—the one that was awkwardly located on the second floor of a building with no elevator.

When we arrived outside the Blue Dolphin, I got behind her on the stairs that her rickety little legs couldn't easily manage. Using our perfected stair maneuver, I pushed up under her bottom and propelled her one stair at a time while she held the railing with both hands. She got her daily belly laugh during that clown show. It worked for us, if not for some onlookers.

We sat at a back table, Mama enjoying her fried fish and coleslaw, using all the salt her heart desired. I couldn't tell which she enjoyed most, her greasy fish and fries or breaking the assisted living contraband rules. She would have what she wanted, even if it meant hiding a saltshaker in the pouch on her walker during the home's meals. She still had that stripe of spunk that made her.

It was a lazy summer afternoon, so after lunch we decided to go to Charles River Park to sit by the river. She had always loved the outdoors, so she relished the chance to sit in the fresh air and enjoy the greenery. I chose that spot where she could also watch the mixed-race world go by.

Mama wheeled her walker around sprawling tree roots and too many goose droppings, passing Harvard students biking and families whose little kids splashed under the wading pool's blue duck fountain. We found a bench to sit on as the gentle pulse of the river flowed by.

There were some older whites sitting together on benches across the walk. When a charcoal-colored girl in a peach skirt strolled by, hand-in-hand with her white boyfriend, I pointed out that none of the elders turned around to give the dirty looks I'd seen too much of all my life. I suggested to Mama that race mixing had become so common that even the old people no longer seemed to notice or care.

Over in the wading pool, we saw children laugh as they conquered the tiny red water slide. A Spanish-accented Big Brother type had several white and black Little Brothers calling to catch the ball. Amerasian sisters in floral swimsuits delicately splashed each other. A white mother toweled off her mixed daughter who had the same kinky-curly hair as mine.

As people enjoyed their summer sun with people from every other tribe, Mama agreed this part of the world was moving on. Nobody out there seemed to care a whit about the diversity of their loves and friendships. "It's beautiful," she said.

A flock of ducks floated near us. They flipped their butts in the air and dunked their heads under water, then came upright again for air. "That's how my work life has been," I told Mama. I spent decades flipping between a more white-like behavior with the corporate types who paid me, then flipping back in private to my black identity where I could breathe easier. It had taken decades to discover and own all of my mixed-race self, to understand it required no label, explanation, or code switching, before I stopped flipping and dipping.

I realized in that moment that was exactly what she had modeled for me. She had presented herself as the white woman she was, not some code switcher. She respected everyone else's humanity and believed that she and her mixed family, just as they were, deserved everyone else's humanity in return.

Mama and I boarded our last flight to Indianapolis in 2005, for her ninety-fifth birthday party at Dorothy's house. It was to be her only celebration with her family of origin in more than sixty years, and Dorothy had made plans with all the Indianapolis family.

Just the two of us went. Daddy, David, and Luther had passed away; Jennifer was studying overseas; and Charles Nathan opted out.

Mama laughed lightheartedly as she angled her walker down the plane aisle like an Olympic Ancient-Walker Champion. Unlike our first trip to Indy, now she was mellow up in the air. No Jack Daniels was needed as she browsed magazines and wondered aloud which in-laws would be at her party.

How much alike we'd become. We'd gone for what we wanted when nobody around us understood. She'd gotten divorced when nobody did, and I left home to go to college when nobody had. We'd both moved hundreds of miles away from family. She moved to get married and I moved to pursue professional advancement. We'd both chosen to cross over into foreign cultures. She lived in the Negro culture, and I lived in the French culture and white corporate America. We had both refused to follow accepted race norms. She married a black man, and I went to find our secret white family. And while our lives had swung between thrills and heartbreaks, both of us had done what we felt we had to. I felt proud of being cut from the same cloth, and filled that our shared journey had led us to this celebration of her.

We landed in Indy and went straight to Aunt Dorothy's downsized two-bedroom duplex in Greenwood in good time to go out to eat. We chose a place for Mama, who was on the hunt for BBQ pork ribs and strawberry pie to fill her cast iron stomach, still able to digest anything.

The next day, August 21, all the relatives in Indy came to Aunt Dorothy's for the potluck party. Except for Uncle Tony, who was recuperating in the hospital but insisted we go on without him. The occasion was too significant to put off, he said. It was special enough to have the Boehles' in-laws and stepchildren we'd shared times with through the years come over, as well as my three cousins who lived there with their own families.

One of Mama's great nephews held her chair at the dining room table for her, and one of my cousins brought her punch. She admired the festive balloons, napkins that read "95th Birthday," and beautifully wrapped gifts that made the room festive. As each person arrived, they added their home cooking to the feast spread out in the kitchen. Antoinette's specialty, corn pudding, was so good I took the recipe for my own parties.

Dorothy said a blessing, then the crowd caught up with each other over dinner. As we talked about Tony coming home soon, one of the boy's plans to join the military, and Jennifer's PhD studies in Africa, it felt as if we'd always been together. Twenty-five years after I first met the Boehles, we were as settled into our blended-race family as any other extended family might be.

"Tell the kids the story of how Mom and Aunt Ella got back together," Judy said to me. Everybody knew the details, including the kids, but it was what brought us all together to celebrate Mama. As I went over the story, people said the way it had changed their lives because the story belonged to everyone there.

"Why did you come looking for us? Judy asked.

Because I needed to know who my family was, I said. So I could find out who all of me was. Because I didn't want race to keep Mama from her people.

Jim, my cousin Darlene's husband, was a man from the heartland who didn't waste words. I'd met him a few times but didn't know him well. "That's how it's supposed to be," he said, touching me deeply. The quiet unassuming man who hadn't commented on our journey all this time, crossed out any complicated angst we'd endured and blessed us by simply saying what we did was right.

After the presents and cake, we went out to the side yard for a group photo. In the bright sunshine we sat the dog between Mama and Dorothy's feet, held up the "95th Birthday" napkins, and shot the picture of a united family that still graces the foyer of my house.

Mama's first birthday with her family in Indy in sixty years.
She was ninety-five. Mama is third from the left in the front row.

After the guests had gone, we went to check on Tony and take him some cake. "Sorry I missed it, Ella," he said. "This was the kind of party you don't hear about every day, and I was glad for you to have it."

Mama and I shared the guest room that night, like always. We crawled into our twin beds under sweetly embroidered new yellow quilts. She turned off the hearing aid that squealed when she touched it and put her false teeth in the blue plastic cup of Efferdent to soak overnight. I reached over and turned off the lamp.

"Today I got my family back," she declared, her speech slushy without teeth to help form the words. "Finally, at ninety-five. And you gave that to me."

Without her hearing aids, she probably couldn't hear me when I said thank you. But Mama had to know telling me that was an equally precious gift.

Just months later, Mama and I spent Christmas week gallivanting through Buffalo wheelchair style to visit still-living friends, eat buttered popcorn before she slept through a movie, and sit in the car watching boys challenge each other in a skatepark bowl.

When I kissed her good-bye on Sunday afternoon, she said it was the best Christmas in years. Then the home called Tuesday morning to tell me a massive stroke during the night had left her unresponsive.

I got to the hospital when there was still time enough for the Catholic priest, who didn't need to know she was excommunicated, to administer the Last Rites. My beloved mother's soul deserved that final blessing from the church her heart had never left, so I gave it to her. Judy came with Dorothy, just a few years before my aunt's death, to help bury Mama.

Mama was laid to rest beside Daddy, under their rose-colored double headstone. She'd chosen it when he died to resemble her own parents' double headstone, the one we prayed over together with Dorothy on that long-ago reunion trip in Indianapolis.

21

LEANING INTO BROWN

Jennifer's Skype call rang one night from St. John's island where she was vacationing with her white boyfriend. They came up on the screen together, looking quite pleased, a festive ocean view restaurant in the background. Noticing her glam earrings, I said, "You're so dressed up for a beach trip."

"Because we got married today!" They grinned at each other, holding their ring fingers up to the camera. Craig panned Jennifer's white dress and tropical bouquet. "Island Mike officiated, here on Trunk Bay. The weather was gorgeous."

"What? What? What?" I said. "You got married?" I paused a minute, trying to get it through my head. "Wow. Well, congratulations." What else could the mother of a thirty-six-year-old college professor say? So, yeah, they were mature enough, compatible, and in love, and had been together for a couple of years. The joy on their faces was everything a parent could hope for.

"We've saved you the price of a big wedding," Jennifer said, laughing. "We didn't want all that. Anyway, the random swimmers and sunbathers out there cheered for us." They'd secretly planned it all—a photographer, a hairdresser, the license in St. Thomas, and the officiant with the best wedding website.

After their continued honeymoon, I arranged a reception in Boston. Craig's parents flew in for the party and Jennifer's new father-in-law

Jennifer and Craig married in 2017.

gave the toast while white and black guests from several generations wished them happiness. Like the 66 percent of Americans who told AARP it was OK for family to marry another race, they were happy for their son.

It was all good until we parents posed for the family picture with the couple. It hurt that none of my family who should have been at such an occasion were there, because they were already gone. Daddy died in 1980, lupus took Luther in 1987; then David, Aunt Dorothy, and Charles Nathan had all died in turn.

But it was Mama I missed most. How I wished the one who had helped raise Jennifer was still alive to see how free her granddaughter was to marry another race. If only Mama could have lived to see that Jennifer did not have to say she was dead and go in hiding for fear of violence against her husband, like Mama did in 1943. There Jennifer stood, her champagne glass aloft as her white father-in-law gave his blessing, crisscrossing the boundary of her white grandmother's foray over the race line. And like her grandmother, Jennifer says her mixed marriage doesn't change her blackness, just the way Mama said her mixed marriage didn't change her whiteness.

I wished Mama could see how alike we three generations had turned out. We were all women who chose to cross over and embrace other cultures, following in her footsteps to sidestep race norms for the lives we wanted.

These days Jennifer and her husband are my window into the millennials who reject race boundaries. Like their mixed peers, they are people who had jobs, educations, or social circles that put them in contact with each other. Like any other couple, their bonds are based on common values, interests, and shared experiences. I know how true that is listening to the animated academic conversations between my daughter and her fellow professor husband in their own language—pedagogy, publishing, and syllabi. And like my mother, their focus is having a loving family.

Some mixed millennials I've spoken with ask, "What is the big deal?," perhaps not understanding the price paid by couples decades ago. Like the black bride who was surprised to learn that my parents couldn't be seen together in public back in 1942 Indiana nor the risks attached if they were.

Black adult children of my friends who chose white spouses have been supported by their parents. Most had "the talk" before the wedding. Do you know what you are getting into? What does his/her family think? Are you sure? Even the parents who secretly acknowledge that they hoped their children would marry black spouses who understood their culture and understood how to maneuver in the white world have stepped over the race barriers with them. They want their children to have happy marriages. They understand times are changing.

It was evident how things were changing when I went to my local community center for a Loving Day party. The hall was full of mixed-race families at the event marking the fiftieth anniversary of the Supreme Court's decision legalizing interracial marriage across

America. So, like the Irish do on St. Patrick's Day, I went to celebrate my own heritage(s).

A woman with skin colored just like mine welcomed me warmly. Somebody asked later if she was my daughter. I wandered about slowly, taking in the Asian, black, Hispanic, Native, and white adults with their blended children of every combination. The variety of skin tones, hair textures, and eye shapes were as familiar as the old Clique Club gang and my own face, like we were all somehow related. It felt good to be surrounded with the normalcy of mixed race when the public had made an issue of it all my life.

It reminded me of what I'd seen on an excursion in Cuba. Dianelys, the Havana tour guide with cream-colored skin, told our group of African American travelers we had a lot in common. She said, like all Cubans, she was *mestizaje*—mixed with African blood. Their 1959 revolution, so the official explanation went, was a racial democracy, where everyone is equally Cuban first and race mixing a part of who they are. That dream, though not completely true, sucked at me like undertow, pulling me to the place I'd never been able to articulate I wanted to see in America.

The same woman who welcomed me to the Loving party had a video camera hoisted on her shoulder, capturing people's family stories on film. When she approached me, I gave the thumbnail of Mama's disappearance and reunion with her family. Others standing nearby smiled. nodding acceptance. Like they knew exactly what my life had been about. Like their own lives were somehow parallels. No questions were necessary about why Mama ran, or how my parents struggled as a mixed couple, the questions whites always ask me. These people already knew. It was my turn to smile, to not feel like a freak with some abnormal life. I relaxed into what I came for, a sense of belonging in my own tribe.

Party organizers began their remarks by announcing that Loving Day was being celebrated that day in cities across the United States. There were family parties like ours going on at much bigger Mixed Remixed Festivals and street happenings in Brooklyn and Los Angeles. There interracial people are so common the press has called them havens.

There were also parties in many unexpected places, like Griffin, Georgia, and Grand Rapids, Michigan.

The speakers painted the picture of America's rising interracialism. First, they cited the 2000 Census, which listed sixty-some race categories that could be mixed for the first time. Before that, I would have fallen into mulatto or quadroon mixed-race Census categories, which were on the forms from 1850 to 1920. Those were designations slave holders and Jim Crow politicians used for decades, lest anyone with black blood pass over into whiteness. In 2000 I had filled in my own Census form by checking both the black and white races, excited that my country had really seen and affirmed me. I was no longer restricted to marking just the box for blacks, in denial of Mama.

I'm in my seventies now, wondering if the United States will ever move past its racial strife and resulting fears about race mixing. It's just so ingrained.

Yet I have seen the perception of race mixing move from illegal and dangerous to a growing demographic today exceeding seventeen million Americans.

My interracial kind can now be found in high places. While enjoying a certain acceptance and even popularity, the mixed-race love my parents helped pioneer in the 1940s has not been fully embraced. Barack Obama was chosen president twice, then rebuked by the election of a racist named Trump. Meghan Markle married into Britain's royal family but faced media backlash, including a family photo portraying their baby as a monkey. Advertising implies the use of mixed-race actors imbue their products and us with some greater common humanity. As if antimiscegenation was never a thing. But, as America would have it, this normalization message is not shown in regions where it might aggravate viewers.

In my family, Jennifer and her husband expect to live their interracial life in peace, because they live in an area where it is not much of an issue. But they are clear-eyed about the fact that brown skin can bring trouble. At one of our Sunday lunches, they agreed to prepare their little mixed-race son for the systematic and interpersonal conflicts he will face.

They plan to teach him how to be safe in this time of police brutality and white terror because mixed people are still black in America. And, like the four generations of my family before him, my grandson will have to face people trying to stop him from naming himself and defining his own place in society.

I have hope because my family, black people and white people together, have embraced love across the color line for the last seventy years. So have the growing millions of other Americans who have discovered that love triumphs over race. While that trend will accelerate, I don't know how far America will move in this direction.

But what I do know is this:

The American identity is in flux, leaning into brown. A significant portion of our citizens will push past the barriers of family racial separation the way Mama, Aunt Dorothy, Jennifer, and I have. Continually growing numbers will look beyond color to marry the partner they love, raise the children they want, and unite with family branches of different races.

And yet, racial strife still dominates American life. I can't see the United States ever adopting the theory of racial democracy the way Cuba espouses, where mixed race is a popular notion. Our intrinsically white supremacist culture, which wants to keep their race pure and in power, makes that clear every day. Because of them, all us mixed, black, and brown families will necessarily protect ourselves by remaining vigilant and fighting everything from microaggressions to police shooting unarmed minorities.

Meanwhile, when my family is together, color is not our focus. Me and mine, and the millions of others who choose mixed-race families, are going to keep on loving.

EPILOGUE

M ama's ninety-fifth birthday party in 2005 made news in her hometown. The *Indianapolis Star* covered her nearly sixty-five years of crossing racial barriers with a front-page story:

LOVE DIVIDED, REUNITED
Woman who gave up family to marry a black man
rejoices in reconnecting with sister she left behind

The article sidebar cited the 2000 US Census report that one in fifteen marriages were then interracial (counting all mixtures, not just black and white), up 65 percent from the prior decade.

Response to the article, the reporter told me, was mixed. There were people who connected to the loving family who looked beyond race, but there were also those still against race mixing who complained about running such a story. The response was a true snapshot of where the country stands—this change in America is happening, though it is still unacceptable to some.

Since my parents threw out the norms and laws to marry in 1943, mixed-race marriage in 2015 was estimated to be at least one of every ten marriages, and according to a PEW Research study, two-thirds of Americans say it "would be fine" with them if a family member married someone of another race.

Now the pace of interracial growth is accelerating. That means this group will get bigger faster. The Census reported that multiracial people grew three times as fast as single-race people between their last two counts. As that trend continues, as new statistics project, mixed-race people will become a notable slice of the American pie when the nation becomes "minority white" in 2045, according to a Brookings Institution study.

If the currently estimated seventeen million mixed-race people were added to seven million so-called white Americans who would be classified as Negroes under the one-drop rule, that would make twenty-five million Americans. So, keep your calculators out. The 2020 Census is predicted to show another significant increase in this growing demographic.

The Loving train is running throughout our country. It's no longer the steam engine my mother fled Indiana on twenty-four years before the Supreme Court overturned antimiscegenation, but a much faster transport heading toward a browner America.

ACKNOWLEDGMENTS

The source material for this book came from face-to-face interviews, some audio taped, videotaped, or handwritten. I am grateful for the heartrending conversations with my family, including my mother and father, Ella and Charles Jackson; my husband, Luther Johnson; Aunt Dorothy and Uncle Tony Boehle and their children.

My brothers Charles Nathan and David spent many hours reconstructing memories and impressions of our mixed-race lives, individually and collectively. There was soul-searching at every turn. I thank them for telling the truth, however painful, in support of this work.

The Clique Club women Sally McCullough (and her husband, Bill) and Marie Crump were an important part of my growing up, and their daughters Valorie Braziel and Diane Crump Richmond generously fleshed out their stories by talking with me for days. Angela Williams; her children, Sandra, Rick, and Robert; her husband, George; her grandson; and her original hometown are all changed names. During lengthy conversations, that family agreed to include their story if they were disguised in some way. That request honors their mother's dying wish not to reveal her double-life secret. These families have been my family and I tried to represent them fairly and truthfully on these pages. I am deeply indebted to all of them for their openness and honesty. I love you all and I feel you.

Say I'm Dead is recreated from collective memories, recounted by those involved or present, and family stories told to us. They have been checked among these parties, their husbands, children, and siblings wherever possible. People in this book do not remember everything, nor do they all remember it exactly the same way. But I did my best to tell what I learned from extensive talks over a decade to capture their experiences in their own words before writing it. Thank you to my mother, "Ella" Jackson, whose work on this project was fundamental in making the story whole. I wish she, my father, my brothers Charles Nathan and David, my husband Luther, Aunt Dorothy, and "Angela" had lived to read it.

Thank you to my agent, Jessica Papin, who believed in my story from the day we met and continued to encourage me. Thank you to my editor, Jerry Pohlen, and all the staff at Chicago Review Press who worked with me to bring this book into the world.

Many thanks to those who helped me put this memoir on the page. Instructors and writing groups at GrubStreet in Boston were instrumental. Special thanks go to Alex Marzano Lesnevich who taught me to write memoir, and those who read the manuscript front to back and offered valuable suggestions: Jonathan Escoffery, Jessamyn Hope, Cindy Layton, Mary C. Curtis, Deborah Schifter, and Priscilla Bourgoine. Thank you to those who started me on my writing path, including my classmates and supportive friends in the WWWA writing group and Memoir Incubator Program.

Much of writing, structure, and editing of *Say I'm Dead* was done during writing residencies that provided the time, space, and solitude to work undisturbed in their studios and nurturing environments. Thank you to Djerassi, Ragdale, the Virginia Center for Creative Arts, Blue Mountain Center, and Wellspring House for those especially productive opportunities.

Thank you to the many personal cheerleaders, too many to name, who encouraged me in this project for years. Chief among them is my daughter, Jennifer E. Johnson, a constant inspiration. Her belief in my work and willing ear throughout the process sustained me through years of work.

QUESTIONS FOR DISCUSSION

1. Understanding one's identity is a major theme of this book. Ella, Dolores, and Jennifer each chose to shape their own identities rather than go along with public norms or perceptions. How do their actions make you feel about them?

2. Dolores found the stranger's question "What are you?" off-putting. Did you ever have that question about someone else? Why is that important to know? Or, has your own identity ever been questioned? Has it shifted based on class, education, immigration, or other reasons? How did it make you feel?

3. Ella breaks Catholic doctrine to remarry and is excommunicated. Yet she continues to turn to God and participate in Catholic practices all her life. What do you think of her actions?

4. Do you think Ella did the right thing running away to marry Charles? Which family was more important, in your opinion, her parents and sister or her husband and children? Why?

5. Did Dolores's need to understand her full racial identity justify the family upset caused by her search for family?

6. How did race pressures affect the life-changing decisions made by Charles, Ella, Dolores, Dorothy, and Jennifer? How were they different for the black, mixed, or white people?

7. Ella's family welcomed her back after a thirty-six-year disappearance. What was it that defined the Boehles' ability to offer such forgiveness?

8. Was Ella right not to make an issue of her mixed marriage with her children? What insights to her character did her actions provide?

9. The term *equal opportunity racism* is used in the book to describe how both blacks and whites acted on racist beliefs. Does this bring to light any prejudices you hold or face?

10. The 1950s TV show *Amos 'n' Andy* was detrimental to blacks' self-image and reinforced whites' negative black stereotypes. While today's media has moved on from such blatant portrayals, are damaging media stereotypes still influencing the public?

11. Is it possible *not* to let race dictate one's life? Is that possibility different for white people versus for people of color? Why or why not?